*The Random House
Large Print Book
• of •
Jokes
• and •
Anecdotes*

The Random House Large Print Book

$\cdot$ of $\cdot$

Jokes

$\cdot$ and $\cdot$

Anecdotes

For Anyone Who Needs a Laugh

Edited by

JOE CLARO

Published by Random House Large Print
in association with Random House, Inc.
New York

Copyright © 1990 by Random House, Inc.

All rights reserved under International
and Pan-American Copyright Conventions.
Published in the United States of America
by Random House Large Print in association
with Random House, Inc., New York,
and simultaneously in Canada
by Random House of Canada Limited, Toronto.
Distributed by Random House, Inc., New York.

Library of Congress Cataloging-in-Publication Data
Random House book of jokes and anecdotes.
The Random House large print book of jokes
and anecdotes : for anyone who needs
a laugh / edited by Joe Claro.
1st large print ed.   p.   cm.
Originally published: The Random House book
of jokes and anecdotes. 1st ed. © 1990.
Includes index.   ISBN 0-679-75693-0
1. American wit and humor.   2. Anecdotes.
I. Claro, Joseph.   II. Title.
[PN6162.R34   1994]   94-22512
818'.02—dc20   CIP

Manufactured in the United States of America
9876543

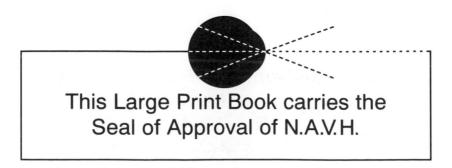

This Large Print Book carries the
Seal of Approval of N.A.V.H.

• *Contents* •

· *Introduction* ·

The Random House Large Print Book of Jokes and Anecdotes will make you laugh; more important, it will help you make your audience laugh.

On the following pages, you'll find nearly one thousand jokes and anecdotes that you can use for any public-speaking occasion. There are icebreakers to warm up your listeners, humorous short tales to liven up your speeches, and witty one-liners to entertain any group. The table of contents and index will help you find material on just about any subject.

But remember, no matter how you use this book, keep this old adage in mind: Laugh and the world laughs with you—just don't do it while unaccompanied in a public place. Solitary public laughers run the risk of ending up in night court.

PART ONE

■

Short Jabs

▲

Playwright Neil Simon has always had mixed feelings about being known as the King of the One-Liners, since his plays are clearly more than collections of punch lines. He once talked about the difficulty of translating some of his material into French, which often requires several more words than the original. "In French," Simon said, "I'm known as the King of the Two-Liners."

Here we present a collection of two-liners and their slightly heftier cousins. For old times' sake, we've also included a small number of one-liners.

We've broken this section down into an alphabetical list of topics, but you'll find that most of the jokes can be used as comments on several subjects.

▼

• *Age* •

"When Abraham Lincoln was your age," the father told his son, "he used to walk ten miles every day to get to school."

"Really?" the kid said. "Well, when he was your age, he was president."

A woman walked up to a little old man rocking in a chair on his porch. "I couldn't help noticing how happy you look," she said. "What's your secret for a long, happy life?"

"I smoke three packs of cigarettes a day," he said. "I also drink a case of whiskey a week, eat fatty foods, and never exercise."

"That's amazing," the woman said. "How old are you?"

"Twenty-six," he said.

A woman got on the bus with her little boy and paid one fare. The bus driver pointed out that she had to pay for her son.

"Children under six ride free," the woman said.

"Come on," the driver said. "He doesn't look a day under nine."

The woman shrugged and said, "Can I help it if he worries a lot?"

• *Animals* •

A cat and her four kittens came face-to-face with a large collie. While the kittens cowered, the cat let out a series of loud barks, scaring the dog away.

Turning to her kittens, the cat said, "You see how important it is to know a second language?"

A male and a female pigeon made a date to meet on a ledge outside the fiftieth floor of the Chrysler Building. The male was there on time, but the female arrived an hour late.

"Where were you?" he cried. "I was worried sick."

"It was such a nice day," she explained, "I decided to walk."

Rhonda walked into her living room and saw her brother playing chess with their dog.

"Amazing!" she sputtered. "This must be the smartest dog in the history of the world!"

"He's not so smart," her brother mumbled. "I've beaten him three out of five games so far."

"Why do you say Rex is a carpenter dog?"
"Last night, he made a bolt for the door."

• *Banking* •

Her teenage son was having trouble mastering the fine points of balancing his new checking account. "The bank returned the check you wrote to the sporting goods store," she said.

"Good," the boy said. "Now I can use it to buy some clothes."

Later, she was trying to explain to him that his account was overdrawn.

"Impossible," her son said. "I still have five checks left."

• *Business* •

Some people who go into business for themselves have more money than brains. But not for long.

Sign in a store window: DON'T BE FOOLED BY IMITATORS CLAIMING TO BE GOING OUT OF BUSINESS. WE'VE BEEN GOING OUT OF BUSINESS LONGER THAN ANYONE ELSE ON THIS BLOCK.

. . .

A man known for his shady business tactics was giving advice to his son, who had just graduated from college. "There are two rules," the man said, "to keep in mind throughout your business career. The first is: When you give your word, always keep it."

"Yes, Dad," the young man said. "And what's the second rule?"

"Don't give your word."

• *Cars* •

Dick Cavett once explained why he doesn't like to drive small sports cars. "Every time I stop at a light, I expect a little kid to come up and say, 'It's my turn.' "

His car was stalled in the middle of a busy street, and the woman behind him honked continuously as he tried to start it up. Finally, he got out and walked to her car.

"I can't seem to get my car started," he said, smiling. "If you'll go and start it for me, I'll stay here and lean on your horn."

A Texas rancher was bragging to the owner of a small farm in Illinois. "I can get in my car at six in the morning," he said, "drive for six hours, spend an hour eating lunch, drive another six hours, and I still wouldn't have reached the end of my property."

"Yeah," the farmer said, nodding sympathetically. "I had a car like that once."

• *Children* •

The four-year-old girl stared at her grandfather for a long time. Then she asked, "Grandpa, were you on Noah's Ark?"

"Of course not," he answered, chuckling.

"Then how come you didn't drown?"

The teacher asked each member of her sixth-grade class to write the names of nine outstanding Americans. Ten minutes later, the teacher saw that everyone but Carl had finished writing.

"What's the matter, Carl?" the teacher asked. "Can't you think of nine great Americans?"

"I have eight," Carl said. "But I still need a second baseman."

On the first day of school, a first grader handed his teacher a note from his mother. The note read, "The opinions expressed by this child are not necessarily those of his parents."

• *Computers* •

The world's first fully computerized airliner was ready
for its maiden flight without pilots or crew. The plane
taxied to the loading area automatically, its doors
opened automatically, the steps came out automatically.
The passengers boarded the plane and took their seats.

The steps retreated automatically, the doors closed,
and the airplane taxied toward the runway.

"Good afternoon, ladies and gentlemen," a voice
intoned. "Welcome to the debut of the world's first
fully computerized airliner. Everything on this aircraft is
run electronically. Just sit back and relax. Nothing can
go wrong . . . nothing can go wrong . . . nothing can go
wrong. . . ."

A man and his wife met at the commuter train for the
ride home. He looked haggard, and she asked, "Did you
have a rough day, dear?"

"You bet I did," he answered. "The computer was
down, and we had to think all day long."

The computer is one of the great inventions of our
time. There are still as many mistakes being made as
ever, but now they're nobody's fault.

A first-grade teacher was overseeing her students as
they experimented with their desk computers. One boy

sat staring at the screen, unsure how to get the computer going. The teacher walked over and read what was on his screen.

In her most reassuring voice, she said, "The computer wants to know what your name is." Then she walked over to the next child.

The boy leaned toward the screen and whispered, "My name is David."

"Just give us a few days," the repair technician said. "When we have the part, our computer will call your home to let you know."

"I'm not home during the day," the customer said. "But I do have an answering machine."

"Sorry, sir," the technician said. "Our computer won't talk to a machine."

Crandall was proud of the efficiency of his completely computerized home. That's why he was so annoyed at what the telephone operator had just told him.

"What do you mean, it's busy?" he sputtered. "I'm calling my coffee maker!"

• *Death* •

Six months after the waiter died, his widow went to see a medium, who promised she would contact the dead man. During the séance, the widow was sure she saw her husband standing in the corner, dressed in his waiter's outfit.

"Arnold!" she cried. "Come closer and speak to me!"

A hoarse voice from the corner wailed, "I can't. It's not my table."

Three men stood before Saint Peter, waiting to be admitted into heaven. "Before you go in," Saint Peter said, "I have to ask you a few questions. First, approximately how much did you earn last year?"

The first man said, "I earned about three hundred thousand dollars. I was an investment banker."

The second man said, "I guess I made about half a million last year. I was in real estate."

The third man said, "I made about eight thousand dollars."

"No kidding?" Saint Peter said. "What shows would I have seen you in?"

• *Driving* •

While driving on a highway, a man strummed a guitar he held in his lap. A policeman pulled him over, got out of the police car, and walked over to the driver.

"Do you know you're a menace to the safety of hundreds of people?" the cop asked.

"No," the driver said. "How does it go?"

• *Eating* •

"Waiter, do you have any wild duck?"
"No, sir. But I can irritate a tame one for you."

"What is this, tea or coffee? It tastes like kerosene."
"It's coffee, madam. Our tea tastes like dishwater."

"I'd like a ham sandwich, please."
"Sorry, sir. The only sandwich we make is the Super Special. It has salami, ham, cheese, pickles, onions, peppers, and lettuce."
"Please, all I want is a ham sandwich."
"OK, sir. CHARLIE, ONE SUPER SPECIAL. HOLD THE SALAMI, CHEESE, PICKLES, ONIONS, PEPPERS, AND LETTUCE."

• *Education* •

"Professor, I did the best I could on this test. I really don't think I deserve a zero."
"Neither do I. But that's the lowest grade I'm allowed to give."

. . .

A professor was complaining about a star athlete who was failing all his courses. "He can see the writing on the wall," the professor said. "The trouble is, he can't read it."

Rodney Dangerfield once talked about how tough his high school was. "In our football games," he said, "after they sacked the quarterback, they went after his family."

• *Fax Machines* •

No matter how much the government fights it, organized crime just seems to get more organized every day. The police pulled in a Mob kingpin recently and reminded him he had the right to make a phone call.

"Just fax the arrest report to my lawyer," the mobster said calmly.

Fax machines can have a great effect on politicians. Somebody just sent a fax message to every member of our state legislature. Each fax message was exactly the same: "The press has found out everything." Both houses of the legislature emptied out within thirty minutes.

• *Fish* •

"Waiter, I don't like the looks of this codfish."

"If you're interested in looks, you should have ordered goldfish."

"Armstrong," the boss said, "I happen to know that the reason you didn't come to work yesterday was that you were out playing golf."

"That's a rotten lie!" Armstrong protested. "And I have the fish to prove it!"

The little kid had been sitting on the pier all morning, watching his motionless fishing line. He was trying to decide whether to call it quits when a woman came by. "Fishing?" she asked.

"No," the kid said, flashing her a nasty look. "Actually, I'm drowning worms."

• *Friends* •

A friend in need is usually a pest.

Help a friend in need and she'll never forget you. Especially when she's in need again.

. . .

"I'm ashamed of you," the mother said. "Fighting with your best friend is a terrible thing to do."

"He threw a rock at me," the boy said. "So I threw one at him."

"When he threw a rock at you, you should have come to me."

"What good would that have done? Your aim isn't nearly as good as mine."

Two old friends met on the street and one invited the other to dinner. "We live in apartment 12B," he said. "Just lean on the bell with your elbow."

"Why should I use my elbow?" the other asked.

"You weren't thinking of coming empty-handed, were you?"

• *Gifts* •

Ronnie had been promised a special surprise for his birthday, and that's just what he got. He stared in awe at the full-grown Saint Bernard that stood in the center of his living room.

The little boy inched up to the dog, walked slowly around it, and looked up into its big, brown eyes. Then he turned to his mother and asked, "Is he for me, or am I for him?"

· · ·

His mother had scrubbed floors to send him through college, and he felt he could never adequately repay her. Now a successful businessman, he sent her gifts from all over the world. While traveling in South America, he found a parrot that could speak six languages and recite long passages from Shakespeare. He knew his mother would love such a bird, and he paid $14,000 for it.

When he got back home, he phoned his mother. "How about that bird I sent you?" he asked.

"Thank you so much," his mother said. "It was delicious."

• *Government* •

Two lions escaped from a zoo near Washington, D.C., and took off in separate directions. Weeks later, they ran into each other in the middle of the night.

"I'm having a terrible time getting food," the first lion said. "How have you been getting along?"

"Just fine," the second lion said. "I found a good hiding place in the Pentagon. I eat one general a week. I figure it'll be years before they notice that anyone is missing."

· · ·

The suave Central American diplomat was talking to the prim and proper Washington hostess. "In my country," he said, "the most popular of all activities is making love."

Shocked, the wide-eyed hostess said, "Oh! Isn't that revolting!"

"No," the diplomat said. "That's our second-favorite activity."

• *Hospital* •

"I'm so worried," the nervous patient said as the nurse plumped up his pillows. "Last week, I read about a man who was in the hospital because of heart trouble and he died of malaria."

"Relax," the nurse said, smiling. "This is a first-rate hospital. When we treat someone for heart trouble, he dies of heart trouble."

• *Hotels* •

Last week, I was in a hotel room so small that when I opened the door, I broke the window.

It was so small I had to use a folding toothbrush.

So small that when I dropped my handkerchief, it became a wall-to-wall carpet.

• • •

The desk clerk asked the newly arrived guest if he wanted a wake-up call in the morning.

"No thank you," the guest said. "I always wake up at six on the dot."

"Really?" the clerk said. "In that case, would you mind giving our operator a call at 6:05?"

• *Insurance* •

Her husband had been insured with a company that prided itself on its speed and efficiency. Less than twenty-four hours after he died, an agent appeared at her home and handed her a check for $200,000.

"He was such a good husband," she sobbed. "Why, I'd give half of this money to have him back right now."

"Don't let me pressure you," the life insurance salesman said. "Sleep on it tonight. If you wake up in the morning, you can give me a call."

• *Jobs* •

A little, withered old man walked into the headquarters of a lumber company in western Canada. "I want a job as a lumberjack," he said.

The foreman politely tried to talk him out of the idea. After all, he was old, small, and much too weak to fell trees. Undaunted, the old man took up an ax and proceeded to chop down a huge tree in record time.

"That's just astounding," the foreman said. "Where did you learn to fell trees like that?"

"Well," the old man said, "you've heard of the Sahara Forest?"

"You mean the Sahara Desert."

"Sure, that's what it's called *now,*" the old man said.

"Your application says you left your last job because of sickness. Could you explain that, please?"

"Certainly. My boss got sick of me."

• *Justice* •

"Why couldn't you two men settle this case out of court?" the judge asked.

"We tried to," one of the men replied. "But the police came and broke it up."

The judge sentenced the racketeer to a twenty-year term. Afterward, she rushed into her chambers, threw off her robe, and headed for the exit.

"What's the matter, Judge?" her assistant asked. "Are you afraid his gang will get you?"

"Don't be silly," the judge said. "I'm going over to rent his apartment."

• *Kindergarten* •

The kindergarten teacher was showing her class an encyclopedia page picturing several national flags. She pointed to the American flag and asked, "What flag is this?"

A little girl called out, "That's the flag of our country."

"Very good," the teacher said. "And what is the name of our country?"

" 'Tis of thee," the girl said confidently.

A boy came home from his first day at kindergarten very excited. "We have a magic TV set in school," he announced.

"What's magic about it?" his father asked.

"No remote control," the child said happily. "You change the channel by turning a dial."

• *Kitchens* •

Henny Youngman: I asked my wife where she wanted to go on her vacation. She said someplace she's never been before. I said, "How about the kitchen?"

. . .

Ted and Norman had been roommates for a week when Ted decided to try his hand at cooking. He served a casserole and explained, "I only know how to cook two things: beef stew and cherry pie."

Norman tasted it and said, "Not bad. But which is it?"

"Waiter, would you get the chef from the kitchen, please?"

"What for, sir?"

"It's this soup. I want to ask him whether I'm supposed to eat it or dip arrows in it."

• *Laziness* •

How lazy is he? Well, I've seen him step into a revolving door and wait.

Lazy? He's sworn never to work during any week that has a Tuesday in it.

When he wakes up more than twice in three days, he considers it insomnia.

The foreman watched a new worker carrying sacks of cement. All the other workers carried two sacks on each trip, but the new man carried one. The foreman asked him why.

"I'm glad you noticed," the new man said. "I guess those other guys are just too lazy to make two trips."

• *Literature* •

After reading *Julius Caesar,* one student complained that a play by Shakespeare is nothing but a lot of famous quotations strung together.

The same student wondered why authors get so excited when their books are selected as Book-of-the-Month Club offerings. "How can anybody make money selling only one book a month?" he asked.

It was another student, though, who wondered why anyone would write a novel when you can buy one for fifteen dollars.

• *Money* •

A building contractor was being paid by the week for a job that was likely to stretch over several months. He approached the owner of the property and held up the check he'd been given.

"This is two hundred dollars less than we agreed on," he said.

"I know," the owner said. "But last week I overpaid you two hundred dollars, and you never complained."

The contractor said, "Well, I don't mind an occasional mistake. But when it gets to be a habit, I feel I have to call it to your attention."

Certain government functionaries contend that Americans are getting stronger. Ten years ago, they point out, it took two people to carry home twenty dollars' worth of groceries. Now a child can do it.

There's only one good thing about inflation. The money you don't have isn't worth as much as it used to be.

• *Music* •

"Doctor, how long will my arm be in this cast?"

"At least six weeks."

"When you remove it, will I be able to play the violin?"

"Of course."

"That's great! I could never play it before."

. . .

The high school glee club was singing a collection of Italian folk songs. A woman in the audience became tearful, and soon she was sobbing quietly.

The man sitting next to her asked, "Are you Italian?"

"No," she said. "I'm the music teacher."

In an act that amazed the audience, a dog sat onstage and played several tunes on a piano. As the audience applauded, a larger dog came onstage, forced the smaller dog from its stool, and led it into the wings.

Backstage, the trainer told the theater manager, "That's his mother. She wants him to give up music and go to law school."

• *Nepotism* •

"Would you tell our viewers, sir, how you got to be president of this company?"

"Gladly. I ran into my father at the watercooler one morning. He took a liking to me and put me in charge of the place."

"This is the last time one of your mistakes is going to cost me money. I don't care if you are my son-in-law. You're fired!"

"Fired? Who are you going to find to fill the vacancy?"

"Don't flatter yourself. You aren't leaving a vacancy."

• *News* •

A reporter from Chicago was visiting an old colleague, who now edited a newspaper in a tiny Vermont town. "I don't see how you do it," the reporter said. "How can you drum up interest in the news when everybody in town knows what everybody else is doing?"

"Sure they know," the editor said, "but they read the paper to see who got caught at it."

"Name names!" the crusty editor insisted to his young reporters. "No story is complete without the names of everyone involved."

The newest member of his staff filed the following report on a local disaster:

Three farms in our area were affected by the severe lightning storm that struck Thursday night. Mr. and Mrs. Alva Todd reported a fire in their barn. Michael Arlington said several trees were knocked down by the violence of the storm. And Fred Morse reported that three of his cows were struck by lightning. Their names were Bessie, Gilda, and Plug.

• *Obsessions* •

"Doctor, you must do something about my husband. He thinks he's a refrigerator."

"That's terrible."

"You're telling me! He sleeps with his mouth open, and the light keeps me awake all night."

• *Overweight* •

His wife looked on as he was being measured for a suit. She watched as the tailor brought the tape measure around her husband's considerable waist.

"Amazing," she said. "A fir tree that wide around would be about ninety feet tall."

The doctor handed her overweight patient a bottle of pills. "Don't take these pills," she said. "Spill them on the floor three times a day and pick them up one by one."

• *Pets* •

A well-dressed woman went into a pet store and headed straight for the bird department. The owner gave her a few minutes to look around, then approached her.

"Can I help you?" he asked.

"Yes," she said. "How much is that green bird in the top cage?"

"Six hundred dollars."

"Fine," she said. "I have my car outside. I'd like you to send me the bill."

"Nothing doing, lady," the owner said. "You take the whole bird or nothing at all."

A professional dog-walker was leading her charge toward the entrance to the park. A man walked up to her and said, "That's a beautiful dog. Does it have a pedigree?"

She raised her eyebrows. "If this dog could talk," she said, "he wouldn't speak to either of us."

• *Phones* •

"Is there a florist in the hotel?" the guest asked. "I want to send flowers to your switchboard operator."

"How nice," the desk clerk said. "She'll be thrilled."

"Thrilled?" the guest sneered. "I thought she was dead."

"Information? I need the number of the Caseway Insurance Company."

"Would you spell that, please?"

"Certainly. C as in *sea*. A as in *aye*. S as in *sea*. E as in *eye*. W as in *why*. A as in *are*. Y as in *you*."

"Just a minute, sir. I'll connect you with my supervisor."

• *Quasimodo* •

Quasimodo hired an assistant to help out with his bell-ringing chores. He explained how to swing the bell clapper, then stressed how important it was to move out of the way before the clapper made its return.

The assistant was careless. He swung the clapper but failed to get out of the way in time. The clapper hit him in the face, and he fell from the tower.

Quasimodo rushed to the street, where a crowd had already gathered. "Do you know this man?" they asked him.

"No," Quasimodo answered. "But his face rings a bell."

• *Quiet* •

The little boy was horsing around in the library. The librarian confronted him and said, "Please be quiet. The people around you can't read."

"They can't?" the boy said. "Then what are they doing in the library?"

Two construction workers were pounding away with jackhammers. The first one stopped and signaled to the other, who also stopped.

"I wish you'd cut out the noise," the first worker said. "It's making me nervous."

"What are you talking about?"

"That humming! You're off-key!"

• *Religion* •

The monks were allowed to speak once a year, and then only for a few minutes. On the appointed day, one young monk said, "I wish we could have seeds in our rye bread."

A year went by, and the day came around again. A different monk said, "I prefer rye bread without seeds."

The following year, a third monk remarked, "I just can't stand this constant bickering."

• *Rural America* •

"What do you raise on this farm?" the traveler asked.

"Cotton, corn, peanuts, and a few other things," the farmer replied.

"It must keep you pretty busy. What time do you go to work in the morning?"

"I don't go to work," the farmer said. "I'm surrounded by it."

A farmer came into the local hardware store and bought a dozen axes at fifty dollars each. He came in and made the same purchase every week for a month. Finally, the store owner asked him what was going on.

"I sell these axes for forty dollars each," the farmer explained.

"That's crazy," the store owner said. "You're losing ten dollars on each ax. What kind of business is that?"

"Lousy business," the farmer replied. "But *anything* beats farming."

A driver pulled up beside a rundown farmhouse. He got out and knocked at the door. A very old woman answered the door, and he asked her for directions to Des Moines.

"Don't know," the woman said.

He got back in his car and pulled away. Then he heard voices. He looked in his rearview mirror and saw the woman and an equally old man waving for him to come back. So he made a U-turn and drove up to them.

"This is my husband," the old woman said. "He doesn't know how to get to Des Moines either."

• Selling •

The real estate agent sat the prospective buyers in front of his desk. Then he smiled and said, "First you folks tell me what you can afford to spend for a co-op. We'll have a big laugh over that. Then we'll get down to business."

The sales manager was wrapping up her pep talk to new staff members. "Just remember this," she said. "Always be sincere, whether you mean it or not."

A woman walked up to the manager of a department store. "Are you hiring any help?" she asked.

"No," he said. "We already have all the staff we need."

"Then would you mind getting someone to wait on me?" she asked.

• Sex Education •

When their son asked about sex, they used the traditional story of the birds and the bees. Their explanation seemed to satisfy him, so they went no further.

Later, parents and son sat watching a movie on

television. In a key scene, a man and a woman embraced, then kissed passionately.

"Mom," the boy said, "is this where he puts the pollen on her?"

"Daddy, where did I come from?" the seven-year-old asked.

It was a moment for which her parents had carefully prepared. They took her into the living room, got out the encyclopedia and several other books, and explained all they thought she should know about sexual attraction, affection, love, and reproduction. Then they both sat back and smiled contentedly.

"Does that answer your question?" her father asked.

"Not really," the little girl said. "Marcia said she came from Detroit. I want to know where I came from."

• *Space Travel* •

The astronaut had just finished his first meal on the moon when it was time for a report back to Houston. When they asked about his meal, the astronaut said, "The food was good. But the place lacks atmosphere."

For an experiment with a new type of spacecraft, NASA went back to one of its tested procedures—using a mouse as the passenger. When the craft returned to earth, the mouse was carefully examined, then returned to its original cage in the lab.

"How was it?" the other mice asked excitedly.

"It was pretty rough," the astronaut mouse replied. "But it's a hell of a lot better than cancer."

• *Taxes* •

A Dutch visitor was explaining to an American how he saw the red, white, and blue of the Netherland flag. "To me," he said, "our flag symbolizes our taxes. We get red when we talk about them, white when we see our tax bills, and blue after they have been paid."

"I know what you mean," the American said. "It's the same here, only we also see stars."

The major difference between death and taxes is that Congress can't make death any worse than it is.

• *Traffic* •

"Your driver's license says you should be wearing glasses," the traffic cop said to the speedster. "Why aren't you wearing them?"

"I have contacts," the speedster said.

"I don't care who you know," the cop said. "You're getting a ticket anyway."

According to a recent study, someone is run over by a car every five minutes in the city. You'd think the guy would have enough sense to get out of the street.

• *Unions* •

"Painting the whole house will cost you four thousand dollars," the contractor said.

"Four thousand dollars!" the homeowner screeched. "I wouldn't pay Picasso that much to paint my house."

"Oh yeah? Well, just let him pick up a brush, and your house will be surrounded by pickets."

At the expensive restaurants in town, the waiters' union has a problem. They called a strike at one of the classiest places in the city, but it was two weeks before any of the customers recognized the difference.

• *Used Cars* •

Nobody knows better than the owner of a used car how hard it is to drive a bargain.

. . .

"Mom, what happens to a car when it's too old to run any more?"

"Someone sells it to your father."

The prospective buyer drove the used car back into the lot after taking it for a test drive. The smiling dealer greeted her as she got out of the car.

"This car," he said, "is a golden opportunity."

"Yes," she said. "I could hear it knocking during the whole drive."

• *Vanity* •

"Hello, Fred. Long time no see. When did you start wearing glasses?"

"I've needed them for a long time, but I just got them this week. I finally reached the stage where my curiosity has outstripped my vanity."

Barbara and Denise were having a rare heart-to-heart talk. "What do you consider your worst vice?" Barbara asked.

"I don't like to admit it," Denise said, "but my worst vice is vanity. Sometimes I sit in front of the mirror and just admire my face."

"I wouldn't worry about it," Barbara said. "That isn't vanity. It's imagination."

• *Voting* •

Two men were stopped by a TV newswoman doing street interviews about the upcoming mayoral election. "I'm not voting for any of the candidates," the first man said. "I don't know any of them."

"I feel the same way," the second man said. "Only I know them all."

One campaign consultant says he doesn't approve of political jokes. He's seen too many of them get elected.

It isn't necessary for a politician to fool all the people all the time. A majority on Election Day is enough.

• *Weather* •

Although he was a qualified meteorologist, Hopkins ran up a terrible record of forecasting for the TV news program. He became something of a local joke when a newspaper began keeping a record of his predictions and showed that he'd been wrong almost three hundred times in a single year. That kind of notoriety was enough to get him fired.

He moved to another part of the country and applied for a similar job. One blank on the job application called for the reason for leaving his previous position.

Hopkins wrote, "The climate didn't agree with me."

In southern California, the weather is pretty much the same throughout the year. How does anyone there get a conversation started?

• *Wills* •

The lawyer was reading the old man's will before a gathering of his survivors. As everyone listened attentively, he read the final paragraph: "And, to my nephew Randolph, who always said I wouldn't remember him in my will—Hello, Randolph."

"Being of sound mind, I spent all my money before my greedy relatives could get their hands on it."

• *Xmas* •

Early in December, Holly opened the door to her apartment and found a greeting card taped to the outside. "Merry Christmas from the custodial staff," it read.

"Nice gesture," she thought. Then, with all she had to do, she forgot about it.

A week later, she came home to find another card taped to her door. This one said, "Merry Christmas from the custodial staff. Second Notice."

Most people go through three Santa Claus stages. First, you believe in Santa Claus. Then, you don't believe in Santa Claus. Finally, you *are* Santa Claus.

• *X Rays* •

"You seem to be recovering," the doctor said. "These X rays show some damage to the bone, but I wouldn't worry about it."

The patient said, "If your bone were damaged, I wouldn't worry about it either."

Examining the X rays, the doctor said, "Not a thing to worry about. You should live to be ninety."

"But Doctor," the patient said, "I am ninety."

"See? I was right," the doctor said.

. . .

Halliday finished dressing and went in to see the doctor for the results of his annual checkup. The news wasn't good.

"But Doctor," Halliday protested, "I can't afford expensive surgery right now. And I certainly can't afford to be out of work for months recuperating. Isn't there something else you can do?"

The doctor shrugged and said, "I guess I could have your X rays retouched."

• *Yanks* •

Porter was known as the Yank pilot, the only American member of an Australian flying club. One day, while flying toward the outback, he lost control of the plane and crash-landed. He was discovered by a rancher, who drove him to a hospital, where it was determined that he had no serious injuries. Porter remained unconscious throughout the whole ordeal.

When he awoke the next day, the Yank saw that he was in a hospital, and he realized he could barely move his heavily bandaged limbs. He blinked at the nurse standing near his bed. Then he asked, "Did they bring me here to die?"

"No," she said cheerily. "They brought you here yesterdie."

• *Youth* •

Memorial Day weekend was coming up, and the nursery school teacher took the opportunity to tell her class about patriotism. "We live in a great country," she said. "One of the things we should be happy about is that, in this country, we are all free."

One little boy came walking up to her from the back of the room. He stood with his hands on his hips and said, *"I'm* not free. I'm four."

Mark Twain once said that at the age of fourteen, he was convinced that his parents were among the stupidest people on the face of the earth. When he reached twenty-one, he was amazed at how much they had learned in only seven short years.

• *Zanies* •

A man went to a psychiatrist's office and sat in a plush chair. He took out a pouch of pipe tobacco and stuffed some into his ear.

Watching this, the doctor said, "It seems you've come to the right place. How can I help you?"

"You can give me a light," the man replied.

. . .

A woman ran into a stationery store and confronted the clerk. "Did you see me come in that door?" she asked breathlessly.

"Yes," said the confused clerk.

"Have you ever seen me before?"

"No, I haven't."

"Then how did you know it was me?"

• *Zoo* •

"My brother was arrested at the zoo this afternoon."

"Arrested? What was he doing?"

"Feeding the pigeons."

"But—what's wrong with that?"

"He was feeding them to the lions."

PART TWO

The American Scene

▲

Comedians and comedy writers are often asked to explain the mysterious process of making people laugh. One question that comes up regularly is "Where do you get ideas for jokes?"

The answer, of course, is that they get their ideas from everywhere. If you're in the business of making people laugh, you'd better be able to find material for laughter in just about anything that catches your attention. Nothing in the life of a humorist is safe; family, friends, sacred institutions, and fears are all legitimate ammunition.

"The American Scene" proves that just about anything can be funny. You'll find a lot to recognize in this section, which includes jokes about families, workplaces, commuters, television, supermarkets, and just about everything else that's part of your daily routine.

▼

The office manager was tearing her hair out. Every computer terminal in the place was lit up, the mainframe was humming comfortably, and everything looked exactly as it had when work had come to an end the night before.

The only trouble was that nothing was working. Seven keyboarders sat idly in front of their terminals, waiting for the service truck to arrive. The office manager imagined dollar bills flying out the window as she paced back and forth impatiently.

At the sound of the approaching elevator, she stopped pacing. The doors slid open, and a smiling technician strolled into the office.

"It's about time!" the office manager cried. "I don't know what's wrong. The mainframe is working, the terminals are on, everything seems to be hooked up properly."

"Then what's the trouble?" the technician asked.

"They type on the keyboards," the manager said petulantly, "and nothing shows up on the screen, nothing prints, NOTHING HAPPENS!"

With a little smile, the technician nodded. He walked over to the mainframe, examined the cable connections, and turned to the office manager. "Got it," he said.

He turned back to the mainframe, reached toward the back of the console, and tapped the machine with the side of his hand.

"It's working!" one of the keyboarders called out.

The manager grinned. "Terrific!" she said. "The man is a genius!" she added, pointing to the technician.

"Glad to be of service," the technician said. "That'll be six hundred dollars."

The office manager stared at him in horror. *"Six hundred dollars!"* she sputtered. "Are you out of your mind? You were here less than thirty seconds. All you did was tap the machine. I won't pay a cent until you give me an itemized bill!"

The technician sighed. He pulled an invoice pad from his pocket, wrote something, tore off the top page, and handed it to the office manager.

"Itemized bill," he said calmly.

The office manager read it aloud:

Tapping the back of the console: $20.00

Knowing where to tap: $580.00

A psychiatrist was in the habit of stopping into a local bar after a day of treating patients. The daily routine never varied. The bartender would greet him with a cheery "Hi, Doc!" The doctor would pull up a stool and say, "The usual, please." And the bartender would serve the doctor his usual.

"The usual" in this case was pretty unusual. It was an odd drink the psychiatrist had learned about during a

stay in Mexico years earlier. The drink was a
daiquiri—an ordinary daiquiri, except for the addition of
a chunk of walnut. No other customer drank this odd
mixture, but the bartender kept a small store of walnuts
handy for the daily order.

One day however, the bartender got careless and ran
out of walnuts. His customer was due in about ten
minutes. The bartender searched the premises and
finally discovered, not what he was looking for, but a
supply of hickory nuts left over from a party. He
decided to make the substitution, hoping the
psychiatrist wouldn't notice the difference.

"Hi, Doc!" he called out as his customer came in.
"The usual, please," the doctor said, seating himself on
his favorite stool. The bartender mixed up the drink,
chopped the hickory nut, added it to the mixture, and
served the glass to his customer. "Enjoy," he said,
pretending an interest in the glasses he was wiping.

He watched the psychiatrist take a sip and saw a
look of perplexity cross the doctor's face. Another sip.
More perplexity. The doctor put down the drink and
waved to the bartender, who smiled and said, "Yes,
Doc?"

"I have a question to ask you," the doctor said.
"Please tell me the truth. Is this or is this not a walnut
daiquiri?"

"Afraid not," the bartender said sheepishly. "Actually,
it's a hickory daiquiri, Doc."

. . .

A third grader came home from school one day looking very confused. "Mom," she said, "Ms. Armstrong says I'm in the class of 1999. Is she right?"

"Yes, she is," her mother replied.

"I don't see how it could be," the girl said. "I've counted everyone in all the third-grade sections, and I don't get past 212."

"You just go ahead," the man in the shopping mall said to his wife. "While you're shopping, I'll browse in the hardware store."

An hour later, she returned and saw him at the checkout counter. The clerk was ringing up the last of a pile of tools and supplies that would fill two wheelbarrows.

"Are you buying all this?" his wife asked incredulously.

"Well, yes," he said, embarrassed. Then, waving his arm toward the interior of the store, he added, "But look at all the stuff I'm leaving behind!"

Ninety-four-year-old Mrs. Hatcher showed up at her lawyer's office one Monday morning. "I want you to begin divorce proceedings," she announced.

The lawyer was aghast. When he regained his composure, he said, "Mrs. Hatcher, you and your husband have been married for over seventy years. What in the world could have happened to make you want to get divorced at this stage in your life?"

Mrs. Hatcher looked him squarely in the eye. She cleared her throat and said, "We wanted to wait until all the children were dead."

A young man drove his minibike into a gas station and dismounted. "I'll need about a pint of gas," he said, "and a few ounces of oil for the motor."

"Certainly, sir," the attendant said. "And would you also like me to cough into your tires?"

Arnold and his wife were cleaning out the attic one day when he came across a ticket from the local shoe repair shop. The date stamped on the ticket showed that it was over eleven years old. They both laughed and tried to remember which of them might have forgotten to pick up a pair of shoes over a decade ago.

"Do you think the shoes will still be in the shop?" Arnold asked.

"Not very likely," his wife said.

"It's worth a try," Arnold said, pocketing the ticket. He went downstairs, hopped into the car, and drove to the store.

With a straight face, he handed the ticket to the man behind the counter. With a face just as straight, the man said, "Just a minute. I'll have to look for these." He disappeared into a dark corner at the back of the shop.

Two minutes later, the man called out, "Here they are!"

"No kidding?" Arnold called back. "That's terrific! Who would have thought they'd still be here after all this time."

The man came back to the counter, empty-handed. "They'll be ready Thursday," he said calmly.

Bailey had left his job as a successful marketing man, determined to find the meaning of life. After six months of reading and meditating, he learned of a lama who had spent the last thirty years alone on the top of a mountain in Tibet. Everything he heard about this holy man convinced Bailey that only by visiting the mountaintop could he learn the true meaning of life.

He sold everything he had, flew to Tibet, and hired a team of guides to lead him to the mountain. They took him halfway up, then explained that he would have to make the rest of the trek by himself.

Obsessed with his goal, Bailey continued on, climbing for hours each day and eating only enough to keep up his strength. After ten days of solitary climbing, he reached the top of the mountain. There, sitting cross-legged and facing the sun, was the lama he had come to see.

He carefully made his way to the holy man's spot, stood in front of him, and made a little bow with his head. The lama looked up at his visitor.

"Sir," Bailey said, "I have sacrificed everything, even risked my life, to reach you. I know you are the only one who can tell me the secret of life."

The lama stared at Bailey for several minutes. Finally, he spoke. "Life," he said hoarsely, "is a stream."

Bailey waited, but the man said nothing more. Then Bailey broke the silence. "What do you mean, 'Life is a stream'?"

The old man raised his eyebrows and shrugged his shoulders. "All right," he said, "life is *not* a stream."

He loved living in Staten Island, but he wasn't crazy about the ferry. Miss a ferry late at night, and you have to spend the next hour or so wandering the deserted streets of lower Manhattan.

So when he spotted a ferry no more than fifteen feet from the dock, he decided he wouldn't subject himself to an hour's wait. He made a running leap and landed on his hands and knees, a little bruised maybe, but safe on deck.

He got up, brushed himself off, and announced proudly to a bystander, "Well, I made that one, didn't I?"

"Sure did," the bystander said. "But you should have waited a minute or two. The ferry is just about to dock."

She was trudging home in the snow after an especially hard day at the office. As she passed one of those all-night food stores, she saw a display of peaches that made her mouth water. Wouldn't her husband be pleased with some juicy, ripe peaches in the dead of winter?

She went into the store and asked about the peaches. "Fifty-five dollars a dozen," said the man behind the counter.

"That's almost five dollars a peach!" she said indignantly. "How can you charge that kind of money for fruit? You should be ashamed of yourself."

The man shrugged and went back to reading his newspaper. She made a move toward the door, then came back to the counter. She reached into her pocket, pulled out a dollar bill, and put it on the counter.

The man looked up and asked, "What's that for, lady?"

"I just stepped on a grape."

A man came into a pet shop carrying a parrot in a bird cage. "I want to return this bird," he said.

The owner sighed at the prospect of facing yet another this-bird-won't-talk complaint. "Sir," he said, "we guarantee that all our parrots *can* talk. However, we can't guarantee *when* they will talk. It's all spelled out on your sales receipt."

"No, no, you don't understand," the customer said. "The bird talks. I just don't like his attitude."

Puzzled, the store owner said, "You're right. I don't understand. Explain it to me."

"I bought the bird a week ago," the customer said.

"Every morning, I'd stand in front of his cage and ask, 'Can you talk?' I did the same thing every evening. For six days, I got no response. Then, this morning, I shouted at the bird, 'CAN YOU TALK, YOU STUPID CREATURE? CAN YOU TALK?' "

The customer glared at the parrot. The owner asked, "So, what happened?"

"That bird looked at me," the customer said, "and said, 'I can talk, all right. Can you fly?' "

"It's time to see how clearly you can think," the teacher said to his class. "Now, listen carefully, and think about what I'm saying. I'm thinking of a person who has the same mother and father as I have. But this person is not my brother and not my sister. Who is it?"

The kids in the class furrowed their brows, scratched their heads, and otherwise showed how hard they were thinking. But no one came up with the right answer.

When everyone in the class had given up, the teacher announced, "The person is me."

Little Geoffrey beamed at learning the answer. "That's a good one," he said to himself. "I'll have to try that on Mom and Dad."

At dinner that night, little Geoffrey repeated the riddle to his parents. "I'm thinking of a person who has the same mother and father as I have," he said. "But this person isn't my brother and isn't my sister. Who is it?"

His parents furrowed their brows, scratched their

heads, and otherwise pretended that they were thinking hard. Then they both said, "I give up. Who is it?"

"It's my teacher," Geoffrey said.

Every workday of the year, Hitchcock rode in his chauffered Rolls-Royce to and from work. One spring morning, he decided to make the drive himself. The chauffer warned him that the gas tank was only half full, and Hitchcock said he'd take care of it.

He drove the car into a service station and pulled up in front of a set of pumps. The attendant came out, looked at the car, and walked to the driver's window.

"The tank is on the other side of the car," the attendant said. "Can you back up and pull it into the other side?"

"Sure," Hitchcock said. "Funny thing. I've had this car for four years, and this is the first time I've put gas in it."

"No kidding?" the attendant said, astounded. "If you can tell me how you do it, we might both be able to get rich."

Texas Jim, the oil billionaire, showed up for his semiannual dental examination. The dentist took a series of X rays, then poked around inside Jim's mouth for several minutes.

"Your teeth are in perfect shape, Jim," the dentist told him. "Not a cavity in sight."

Jim looked thoughtfully at him. "Drill anyway," he said. "I feel lucky today."

"That tooth is going to have to come out," the dentist said to his patient.

"How much will it cost?" the patient asked.

"That's an odd question to ask about an infected tooth," the dentist said.

"How much?" the patient repeated.

"Seventy-five dollars," the dentist answered.

Sitting bolt upright, the patient blurted, "What? Seventy-five dollars? For a minute's work? That's highway robbery!"

"Well," the dentist said calmly, "if it will make you feel any better, I can extract it very, very slowly."

Sherry, one of the thousands of unemployed actors in New York City, sat in the anteroom of a photographer's studio, waiting for her pictures. A young man came in, sat opposite her, and struck up a conversation.

"What kind of work do you do?" he asked.

"I'm an actor," she said.

"No kidding?" he beamed. "Which restaurant?"

George had spent a week visiting with his brother. His sister-in-law and his teenage niece accompanied him to the airport for his flight back home. After verifying his seat number, George rejoined them and explained that he'd have to wait an additional two hours.

"How come?" his niece asked.

"My plane has been grounded," he explained.

"Grounded?" his niece said. "I didn't know planes had parents."

"Hello?" the teenage boy said into the phone.

"Hello," a friendly voice said. "This is the National Survey Company. I'd like to ask some questions about the radio programs you listen to."

"Sure," the young man said.

"Do you have the radio on right now?"

"Yes, I do."

"Is anyone else listening with you?" the pollster asked.

"Yes. My father is here with me."

"What are you listening to?"

"My father," the boy said with a sigh.

The manager of a large city zoo was drafting a letter to order a pair of animals. He sat at his word processor and typed the following sentence: "I would like to place an order for two mongooses, to be delivered at your earliest convenience."

He stared at the screen, focusing on that odd word *mongooses*. Then he deleted the word and added another, so that the sentence now read: "I would like to place an order for two mongeese, to be delivered at your earliest convenience."

Again he stared at the screen, this time focusing on

the new word, which seemed just as odd as the original one. Finally, he deleted the whole sentence and started all over. "Everyone knows no full-stocked zoo should be without a mongoose," he typed. "Please send us two of them."

"Can I have a cigarette?" Rosa asked.

"I thought you quit smoking," Agnes said.

"I'm in the process of quitting," Rosa said. "Right now, I'm in the middle of phase one."

"What's phase one?" Agnes asked.

"I've quit buying."

The man sitting in the therapist's office was complaining about an obsession that was ruining his life.

"It's baseball, Doctor," he said. "Please help me. Baseball is destroying me. I can't even get away from it in my sleep. As soon as I close my eyes, I'm out there chasing a fly ball or running around the bases. When I wake up, I'm more tired than I was when I went to bed. What am I going to do?"

The therapist sat back and folded her hands. "First of all," she said, "you have to make a conscious effort *not* to dream about baseball. For example, when you close your eyes, try to imagine that you're at a party at which someone is about to give you several million dollars."

"Are you crazy, Doctor?" the patient shouted. "I'll miss my turn at bat!"

. . .

McWilliams was driving along a narrow country road when his engine simply stopped running. He got out of the car and opened the hood. Since he was anything but an expert on cars, he stared at the engine for several seconds. Suddenly, he heard a voice behind him.

"It's the fuel-injection system," the voice said.

McWilliams turned and saw no one. The only sign of life was a cow standing on the other side of a fence. McWilliams looked around. Then the cow repeated, "It's the fuel-injection system."

McWilliams stared, his eyes widening and his mouth dropping open. "Why are you standing there looking like a fool?" the cow said. "Check the fuel injectors."

McWilliams backed away and swallowed hard. Then he ran up a path that led to a farmhouse at the top of a hill. He pounded on the door until a man opened it.

"Calm down, mister," the man said. "What seems to be the trouble?"

"My car . . ." McWilliams stammered. "My car broke down. I got out to look at the car . . ."

"Yes?" the man said impatiently.

"Your cow!" McWilliams sputtered. "Your cow said to me, 'It's the fuel-injection system'!"

"Ignore it," the man said calmly. "That animal doesn't know a thing about cars."

Bert and Harry went into a diner that looked as though it had seen better days. As they slid into a booth, Bert wiped some crumbs from the seat. Then he took a napkin and wiped some moisture from the table. The waitress came and asked if they wanted menus.

"No thanks," Harry said. "I'll just have a cup of black coffee."

"I'll have black coffee, too," Bert said. "And please make sure the cup is clean."

The waitress shot him a nasty look. She turned and marched into the kitchen. Two minutes later, she was back.

"Two cups of black coffee," she announced. "Which one of you wanted the clean cup?"

"Denise," Laura said, "I have two tickets to the gag-writers' convention. Come with me and you'll see how funny they can be when they get together."

They arrived at a large auditorium just in time to see one of the gag writers step onto the stage. He walked to the microphone and said, "Eighty-seven." The audience broke into peals of laughter.

A second writer walked up to the mike. "One hundred and twelve," she said. Hysterical laughter from the audience.

A third writer said, "Eighteen." The laughter began mildly, then built into a roaring crescendo.

Mystified, Denise turned to Laura and asked, "All right, what's going on here?"

"These are comedy writers," Laura explained. "They know all the good jokes that have ever been told, and they've assigned numbers to the best ones. All they have to do is call out a number and everyone in the audience remembers the joke."

"That's a pretty easy way to get a laugh," Denise said.

"Well—," Laura began, but Denise was already on her way up to the stage. She strode right up to the microphone, cleared her throat, and announced, "Sixteen."

Dead silence. Denise looked around at the sober-faced audience. "Uh—ninety-two," she said, a little uncertainly.

If there had been crickets in the room, their chirping would have been deafening.

Close to panic, Denise called out, "Sixty-three! Ninety-two! Eighty-six!"

The only sound in the room was the clicking of her heels as she scurried off the stage. Laura was waiting in the wings.

"I tried to stop you, Denise," she said.

"What happened?" Denise cried. "I did exactly what those other people had done! Why didn't anyone laugh?"

"I guess it's all in the delivery," Laura said.

Mr. Swiller was known far and wide as a hard-nosed boss who watched his employees like a hawk. He was making one of his regular tours of the factory when he spotted a young man leaning against a pile of boxes just outside the foreman's office. Since George, the foreman, wasn't around, Swiller stood off to the side and watched to see just how long the young man would stand around doing nothing.

The young man yawned, scratched his head, looked at his watch, and sat on the floor. He took out a nail file and began cleaning his nails. Then he stretched, yawned again, and leaned back on the pile of boxes.

Swiller stepped from his hiding place and walked up to the young man. "You!" he boomed. "How much do you make a week?"

The young man looked up indifferently. "A hundred and fifty dollars," he said.

Swiller swooped into the cashier's office, took a $150 from the cash box, and returned. "Take it," he said, "and get out! Don't let me see you around here again!"

The young man took the cash, put it in his pocket, and left. Swiller snorted at his lack of remorse, embarrassment, or any other feeling. Then he went looking for George. When he found him, Swiller was red with anger.

"That idler in front of your office," Swiller said. "I just gave him a week's pay and fired him. What's the matter with you, letting him stand around as though he had nothing to do?"

"You mean the kid in the red shirt?" George asked.

"Yes! The kid in the red shirt!"

"He was waiting for the twenty dollars we owe him for lunch," George said. "He works for the coffee shop around the corner."

. .

The police had finally figured out the modus operandi of a gang of jewel thieves that had been robbing apartments on the east side of town. The thieves had gathered information through their front organization, the Bide-A-Wee Child Care Service.

Bide-A-Wee supplied young women as baby-sitters to their east-side clients. The baby-sitter would size up the apartment and supply information about where the occupants stashed their money and valuables. Several days after the baby-sitter first arrived, the apartment would be robbed.

When they had enough information to make a case, the police raided the Bide-A-Wee offices. In addition to several young women waiting for baby-sitting assignments, the police found a number of well-known local burglars. Detective Randolph, in charge of the operation, barked out orders to the uniformed police officers who made up the raiding party.

"We'll do the premises after we get all these people to the station house," he said. "First, I want you to search every crook and nanny in the place."

Little Deirdre was diligently—but not very successfully—practicing her piano assignments while her mother caught up on some office work in the living room. The doorbell rang, and her mother went to answer it.

A very young policeman stood in the hall, looking more than a little embarrassed. "Mrs. Angler?" he said sheepishly. "Excuse me, but I have to investigate a report filed by one of your neighbors."

"A report?" Mrs. Angler said. "About this apartment?"

"I'm afraid so, ma'am," he said. "Your neighbor swore that somebody named Chopin was being murdered in here."

Peters was in his senior year at a college with a shady reputation. He was the star of the basketball team, which was being investigated by half a dozen state and national organizations. The coach was worried about Peters, who wasn't playing up to his usual standard.

"What's troubling him?" he asked his assistant. "His mind always seems to be somewhere else."

"It's his family," the assistant explained. "His father keeps writing to ask for money."

At that same college, the new dean responded to the investigations by suspending any basketball player who wasn't maintaining a passing average. Furious, the coach came storming into the dean's office, followed by one of his star players.

"You can't keep him from playing!" the coach roared. "We won't win this weekend without him!"

"I don't care," the dean said. "Things have gotten out of hand at this college."

"What do you mean, out of hand?" the coach demanded.

"I'll show you what I mean," the dean said. He turned to the basketball player and said, "Tell me, how much is six times seven?"

The player thought for several seconds. Then he said, "Thirty-one?"

The dean turned to the coach and said, "I rest my case."

"Oh, come on now," the coach said. "Why are you making such a big deal of it? After all, he only missed it by one."

Harrigan squeezed onto the crowded bus and prepared himself for a long, unpleasant ride to work. After a few stops, he found himself in the center of the bus, holding on to the overhead rail to keep his balance. He looked down at the man seated in front of him. The man had buried his face in his arms. He remained in that position as the bus lurched forward.

Harrigan leaned over and asked, "Can I help you? Are you feeling sick?"

"No, no," the man said, his face still buried. "I just hate to see old ladies standing while I sit."

The Michaels family owned a small farm in Canada, just yards away from the North Dakota border. Their land had been the subject of a minor dispute between the United States and Canada for generations. Mrs. Michaels, who had just celebrated her ninetieth birthday, lived on the farm with her son and three grandchildren.

One day, her son came into her room holding a letter. "I just got some news, Mom," he said. "The government has come to an agreement with the people in Washington. They've decided that our land is really part of the United States. We have the right to approve or disapprove of the agreement. What do you think?"

"What do I think?" his mother said. "Jump at it! Call them right now and tell them we accept! I don't think I could stand another one of those Canadian winters!"

Alan, a budding research scientist in junior high school, was conducting an experiment on a grasshopper for his biology class. He put the grasshopper on a table, leaned down until his face was inches away from the insect, and screamed, "JUMP!" The grasshopper leapt into the air.

Alan carefully removed one of the insect's legs. Then he leaned down and once again screamed "JUMP!" The grasshopper responded as before.

Alan repeated this process four more times, each time removing one of the grasshopper's legs. Each time, the grasshopper leapt into the air, though each leap was less impressive than the one before.

Finally, Alan removed the last leg. Then he leaned down and screamed one more time. The grasshopper didn't move. Satisfied, Alan opened his journal and entered the results of his experiment. As a conclusion, he wrote, "When all six legs have been removed, the grasshopper becomes deaf."

A famous concert violinist was relaxing after a performance when a man burst into her dressing room. "Who are you?" she asked angrily. "How did you get in here? No one is allowed in without special permission."

"Please forgive me," the man said. "I know this is an intrusion. But I just have to tell you about my son. He's been playing the violin since he was six, and you'll be amazed at how good he is."

"I'm sorry," the violinist said. "I have a rule against helping musicians I don't know. If I help one, I'll be bothered by people for the rest of my life."

"I know, I know," the man said. "And I understand. But you've never heard anyone play like my son."

The violinist resisted. The father persisted. Finally she agreed to listen, just to get rid of the man. He took out a tape recorder, put a cassette into it, and turned it on.

The violinist listened, enraptured by what she heard. When the tape was finished, she whispered, "That was beautiful. Your son plays like Itzhak Perlman."

"That was Itzhak Perlman," the father said. "But my son plays just like him."

"Mom," the little girl said, "do all fairy tales begin with 'Once upon a time'?"

"No, dear," her mother said. "Sometimes they begin

with 'The couch you ordered has arrived at our warehouse and should be delivered within five working days.' "

Daniels was in Atlanta for her annual visit to company headquarters. She left the hotel, climbed into a cab, and gave the driver the address of the main building. As he pulled out from his parking space, the driver held his left hand out the window and snapped his fingers four times.

Two blocks later, Daniels watched as the driver repeated the strange action. He poked his hand out the window and snapped his fingers four times.

By the time they reached company headquarters, the driver had repeated the ritual about two dozen times. As Daniels handed him the money for the fare, she said, "Listen, I can't leave without asking you. What is all that finger snapping about?"

When he handed over her change, the driver turned to face her. For the first time, Daniels noticed that he had a wild gleam in his eye. "Keeps the Bengal tigers away," he said.

"I beg your pardon?" Daniels said.

"I snap my fingers," the driver said, "because it keeps the Bengal tigers away."

"What are you talking about?" she huffed. "This is Atlanta, Georgia. There are no Bengal tigers around here."

"See?" he said triumphantly. "It works."

. . .

"Information. Can I help you?"

"I'd like the telephone number of the Theater Guild, please."

"One moment, please." Pause. "I'm sorry, sir. I have no listing for Theodore Guild."

"No, no. It isn't a person. It's an organization. It's *Theater Guild.*"

"I told you, sir, I have no listing for a Theodore Guild."

"Not Theodore! *Theater!* The word is *theater!* T-H-E-A-T-E-R!"

"That, sir, is not the way Theodore is spelled."

Harding returned from a two-week business trip exhausted and eager for a hot shower and a relaxing evening. His wife greeted him, took his suitcase and slid it into a closet, and brought him a cool drink.

"How was the trip?" she asked.

"Don't even ask," he said, sipping his drink. Then he looked around the room, hoping to spot his dog. "Where's King?" he inquired.

His wife took a deep breath, folded her hands in front of her, and said, "I'm sorry, dear. King was killed by a truck yesterday."

Harding leapt from his chair, spilling his drink on the rug. "What . . . what . . ." he sputtered. "What kind of a way is that to tell me such bad news? I mean, you've had a whole day to prepare yourself. Couldn't you have tried to soften it a little?"

"But how?" Mrs. Harding pleaded.

"Well, I don't know," her husband said. "You could have prepared me for it, instead of just blurting it out. You might have said, 'King was playing in the street. The neighbor's children were running with him and laughing. Then, all of a sudden, from out of nowhere, a huge truck came roaring down the street.' You could have prepared some story like that, just to cushion the shock a bit."

"I guess you're right," his wife said apologetically. "I'm sorry, dear. I was so upset myself that I didn't think much about how you would react."

Calmer now, Harding said, "That's all right. It's just such a shock, being told right out like that."

He sat back down in the chair and sighed. "I think we should go out for dinner tonight. By the way, where's Mother?"

Mrs. Harding hesitated. Then she said, "Well, she was playing in the street. The neighbor's children . . ."

Ottinger, the governor's most trusted assistant, died in his sleep one night. The governor had depended on Ottinger for advice on every subject, from pending bills to wardrobe decisions. In addition, Ottinger had been his closest friend.

So it was understandable that the governor didn't take kindly to the droves of ambitious office seekers who wanted Ottinger's job. "They don't even have the decency to wait until the man is buried," the governor muttered.

At the funeral, one eager beaver made his way to the governor's side. "Governor," the man said, "is there a chance that I could take Ottinger's place?"

"Certainly," the governor replied. "But you'd better hurry. I think the undertaker is almost finished."

A fisherman was carrying his gear from his cabin to his car, getting ready for the Sunday-evening drive home. A friendly looking man ambled up and asked, "Any luck today?"

"No," the fisherman said. "Today was bad. But yesterday! I caught sixteen trout before lunch, then another dozen in the afternoon. Best fishing day I've ever had."

"No kidding?" the stranger said. "Do you know who I am?"

"Why no, I don't," the fisherman answered.

"I'm the game warden," the stranger said.

"Oh. Well, do you know who I am?" the fisherman asked.

"No, I don't."

"I'm the biggest liar in the United States."

A man came into a bakery and looked around. "Can I help you, sir?" the baker asked.

"Yes," the man said. "I want a special cake made up to celebrate a birthday. I want devil's food cake with white icing."

"That's no problem," the baker said.

"But this cake has to be special," the man said. "It has to be shaped like the letter *G.*"

"That's a little more difficult," the baker said. "But we can do it."

"Good," the man said. "Can I pick it up at noon tomorrow?"

"It will be ready at noon," the baker said pleasantly.

The next day at noon, the customer came back. The baker went into the back and returned with a large cake in the shape of the letter *G.* The customer looked at it and frowned.

"That's all wrong!" he said. "That's a printed letter *G.* I wanted it in the shape of a script letter."

"I'm terribly sorry," the baker said. "I must have misunderstood. But we want our customers to be satisfied. I'll bake you another cake."

"Can you have it ready by three o'clock?" the customer asked.

"That doesn't give us much time," the baker said. "But yes, I'll have it ready for you."

"This time," the customer said, "make sure you get it right."

At three o'clock, the man was back. The baker carried the new cake out to him. The man smiled.

"That's exactly what I had in mind," he said.

"Wonderful!" the baker said, pleased with himself

and the cake he had constructed. "Wait a minute and I'll wrap it for you."

"Don't bother," the man said. "I'll eat it here."

The same baker had to deal with a woman who came in and examined the seeded rolls. "How much are these rolls?" she asked.

"Forty cents each," the baker replied.

"Forty cents!" she said. "The baker on the next block sells the same rolls for thirty cents."

"Yes, ma'am," the baker said wearily. "Why don't you go to the baker on the next block and buy his rolls?"

"I've just been there," she said. "They're out of seeded rolls."

"Oh," the baker said. "Well, when we're out of them, our price is only a dime."

A woman listened while her teenage granddaughter talked about the movie she had just seen.

"The movie was pretty neat. It had a neat story about these people who were going to hold up a bank. The bank was owned by a lousy miser, so robbing him would be a neat thing to do. Then there was this neat chase scene just before the end. I liked the whole thing, except for the music. I think it was classical or something. Whatever it was, it was really lousy."

"You know," her grandmother said, "there are two

words I wish you would stop using. One of them is *neat,* and the other is *lousy.*"

"OK," said the girl. "What are the words?"

A farmer stood leaning on a fence at the edge of his property. He watched as a red sports car came over the top of a hill and followed the road up to the spot where he stood. The driver pulled over to the side of the road and called out to the farmer.

"Do you know how I can get to Route 91?" the driver asked.

The farmer thought for a few seconds. Then he said, "Nope."

"Do you know where the nearest turnpike entrance is?" the driver asked.

"Nope."

"How about the town of Hadley. Do you know which direction it is from here?"

"Nope."

Exasperated, the driver raced his engine. "You don't know very much, do you?" he said.

"Nope," the farmer replied. "But I'm not lost."

Gould and Elliot worked for competing advertising agencies. In fact, each was currently working on a new campaign for a different toothpaste. Elliot, fearful for his job, would have given anything to find out what kind of campaign Gould's agency was planning. That's why he had invited Gould to lunch at one of the city's most expensive restaurants.

"Toothpaste!" Elliot exclaimed. "Who will ever come up with a really original idea for selling toothpaste? By the way, what kind of campaign do you guys have in mind for the Bright-O account?"

Gould looked over his left shoulder, then over his right. He bent forward and whispered, "Can you keep a secret?"

"Yes!" Elliot said in anticipation. "I can really keep a secret."

Gould leaned back and smiled. "So can I."

▶ To end "The American Scene," we've chosen a story based on an old native American legend. Some have called this the worst joke ever told. In the interest of impartiality, we intend to let you be the judge of that.

Long ago, before the land and its animals were ravaged by the robber barons, there lived two tribes on opposite sides of a beautiful, yet sometimes dangerous, lake. These tribes were at war with each other—had been at war for as long as any living member of either tribe could remember.

One day during an especially beautiful spring, a brave from one tribe and a maiden from the other came upon each other in the forest. Recognizing the brave's clothing, the maiden was sure that she was about to be killed. But she soon realized that this was not to be. Instead, the brave marveled over her beauty and the graceful way she moved through the woods, like a young deer.

They talked. They walked through the forest. They shared childhood memories with each other. By nightfall, they were deeply in love. Both were saddened when they had to part. The maiden went back to her tribe, the brave to his, and neither would have dreamed of telling anyone of what had happened in the forest.

They had, however, made a promise. On the night of each full moon, the brave would paddle across the lake. The maiden would be waiting for him on the other side.

They kept their promise through the many full moons. Each time, he would dig out his hidden canoe and paddle across the water. Each time, she would be waiting for him. And each time, they would spend the night looking at the moon and the stars and dreaming of the day when their tribes would allow them to be together forever.

Then, one night, the unthinkable happened. The brave arrived at his hiding place and found his canoe gone. He searched all over, but to no avail. What was he to do? His love would be waiting for him. He could not disappoint her.

He realized there was only one action for him to take. He leapt into the lake and began to swim.

The lake was wide, and the waters were cold, but the brave swam on and on. Eventually, he passed the middle of the lake, and he could see his love on the opposite bank. She waved to him, hoping to give him the strength he needed to reach her.

Then she saw him begin to slow. Soon he was faltering. Long before he reached her, the brave went under.

The maiden vowed then and there that she would never love another. She would devote her life to the memory of the man whose name her tribe had forbidden her to utter.

According to the legend, the lake was named after the man who gave his life to reach the woman he loved.

It is called Lake Stupid.

PART THREE

Occupations and Professions

▲

We've assembled a gaggle of jokes here about various lines of work. You might think of this section as a collection of highly specialized insults.

▼

• *Accountants* •

Wigley had worked for Toney Products ever since he'd received his accounting degree. Now, six years later, he was in charge of his department.

He was a quiet man who did his work and rarely socialized with the other employees. No one particularly liked or disliked him, but he was the subject of constant conjecture by his co-workers, who loved to speculate about his one puzzling habit.

Every morning, he would come into his office, unlock the top drawer of his desk, peek inside, and relock the drawer. Every single morning—the routine never varied. Once he had peeked into the drawer, he might sip his coffee, or open his window, or make a phone call. But nothing happened until he had checked inside that drawer.

Dozens of stories were constructed about the possible contents of Wigley's drawer. Whenever things became boring in the office, the topic of Wigley's drawer was sure to come up, and the latest imaginative possibilities would be explored. But no one could ever do more than guess what he had inside that locked drawer.

Then one night, Wigley left the drawer unlocked. Not only unlocked, but wide open for all to see. Wigley had left early to catch a flight to an accountant's convention. Two hours later, one of the bookkeepers noticed the open drawer. In seconds, the word had spread throughout the office. By the time the bookeeper was making his way to Wigley's desk, his audience had swelled to more than thirty people.

He stepped into Wigley's office, strode over to the desk, and looked inside the mysterious drawer. It seemed to be empty. Then the bookkeeper noticed it. Pasted to the bottom of the drawer was a white piece of paper with a single sentence printed on it.

As his eager audience listened, the bookkeeper read the sentence aloud: "The debit side is the side near the window."

Fresh out of business school, the young man answered a want ad for an accountant. Now he was being interviewed by a very nervous man who ran a small business that he had started himself.

"I need someone with an accounting degree," the man said. "But mainly, I'm looking for someone to do my worrying for me."

"Excuse me?" the accountant said.

"I worry about a lot of things," the man said. "But I don't want to have to worry about money. Your job will be to take all the money worries off my back."

"I see," the accountant said. "And how much does the job pay?"

"I'll start you at eighty thousand."

"Eighty thousand dollars!" the accountant exclaimed.

"How can such a small business afford a sum like that?"

"That," the owner said, "is your first worry."

• *Actors* •

The theater was packed, everyone feeling lucky to be able to get tickets to the closing performance of *King Lear*. The star was a famous British actor whose advanced age made it possible that he might never again appear in an American theater.

His performance was masterly, in spite of a silly little man in a front row who didn't seem to understand the protocol of watching a live performance. Throughout the entire play, the man chattered to his companion, commenting on Shakespeare's dialogue, on the performance, and even on the air-conditioning in the theater. Everyone on the stage was distracted by the man, but all remained unflustered and earned a standing ovation from the audience.

To mark his final performance, the star made a short speech, expressing his gratitude to the audience and praising the actors who had worked with him. Then he turned a fierce glare on the silly little man.

"In conclusion," the great actor said, "I would like to take this opportunity to thank the gentleman in the front row for the privilege of costarring with him all evening."

. . .

It would probably qualify as an off-off-off-Broadway production, but the actors were always hopeful that some influential critic or producer would show up and open the gates to stardom. At five minutes to curtain, the star looked out through a peephole to size up the audience. One of the other actors came up behind her and asked, "How does it look?"

"They all seem to be settled," she said. "But don't worry, it looks as though we still outnumber them."

The producer rolled her eyes as the egocentric actor ranted about his billing in newspaper ads for the show. "If this play is a hit," the actor proclaimed, "it will be because of *my* acting, *my* presence, not to mention *my* name and reputation!"

"Contractual obligations," the producer explained calmly, "force us to give the title of the play first, followed by the author's name, then by the name of Ms. Dunham, who is after all the star of the play."

"Yes, yes, I know," the actor said. "But after that, you should have my name, preceded by AND in capital letters."

"AND?" the producer asked. "Actually, it might be more appropriate if we used BUT."

He was a famous Shakespearean actor, but his wife had been unknown to the public. Some said she hadn't even been very well known to him, since he spent most of his life touring and showed little interest in home or family.

As her casket was lowered into its grave, he was overtaken by tears and sobbing, and he had to be helped into his car. A friend waiting there for him said, "I had no idea you felt so strongly about her. I've never seen anyone so overcome with grief."

The actor dried his eyes and said, "That was nothing. You should have caught me at the funeral home."

"So, you're an actor? I'm a banker myself. I don't get to the theater more than once or twice a year."

"That's about how often I get to see the inside of my bank."

The undertaker stood in the doorway at the actor's funeral, pleased with the way everything was going. The actor's agent came and stood beside him.

"He must have been a greatly admired man," the undertaker said. "So many people have come to pay their respects."

"Yeah," the agent said. "If he'd known he'd have a crowd like this, he would have died years ago."

• *Artists* •

Walpole had lived in his loft for six months, and by now it was filled with the paintings he had created. He worked day and night, stopping only occasionally for something to eat. He thought little about food and less about sleep. But what he thought about least of all was his rent.

As a result, his landlord now stood before him, demanding the three months' rent Walpole owed on the loft.

"Give me a couple of weeks," Walpole pleaded. "I know I'm on the verge of making some sales."

"Absolutely not," the landlord said. "You gave me that story last month. You won't get another day's credit from me."

"Look," Walpole said, "think of it as an investment. Someday this loft will be famous, and you'll be able to charge a fortune for it. In a few years, people will come into this disgusting loft and whisper, 'Walpole used to paint here.'"

"Pay your rent now," the landlord said, "or they'll be able to say it tomorrow morning."

The police were investigating the burglary of the studio of an abstract artist. "So you got a good look at the guy as he was leaving?" one police officer asked.

"That's right," the artist said.

"Can you describe him?"

"I'll do better than that," the artist said. "I'll draw you a picture of him."

Using the artist's rendering, the police went out and arrested a Ford station wagon and two fire hydrants.

. . .

"I won't pay you a nickel for this portrait!" the outraged client sputtered. "Why—I look like a gorilla!"

"You should have thought of that before you hired me," said the artist.

• *Barbers* •

Harry was probably the most offensive barber on the west side of town. He never considered the effect his comments might have on a customer, and he never knew when to hold his tongue.

"Where are you going on your vacation?" he asked as he trimmed behind Mr. Boxer's ear.

"London," Boxer said.

"London!" Harry snorted. "What a dumb place to go on a vacation. Fog and rain, rain and fog. And the food! The term 'English cuisine' is about as meaningful as 'Iranian erotic literature.' Why don't you just burn the money and stay home? Save yourself a lot of trouble."

Like many of Harry's customers, Boxer left fuming. Three weeks later, he was back for another haircut.

"How'd you like London?" Harry sneered, draping a cover over his customer.

"It was wonderful," Boxer said. "We went to Buckingham Palace."

"Sure," Harry said. "With a couple of hundred other dumb tourists."

"No," Boxer said quietly. "It was just my wife and I. We went as private guests."

"You mean you had to pay somebody to let you go in without a tour?" Harry said with a smirk.

"Not at all. We were invited. We got to see the queen."

"Sure," Harry said. "She walked by while you watched from a stairway or something, right?"

"Wrong. We had tea with her and two of her personal assistants."

For the first time, Harry hesitated. Then he charged again. "I'm sure it was a real intimate visit," he sneered.

"As a matter of fact," Boxer said, "the queen leaned over and asked me a very personal question."

"No kidding?" Harry said, his eyes widening. "What did she ask you?"

"She said, 'Mr. Boxer, where on earth did you get that stupid haircut?' "

Barber: Did you have ketchup with your lunch, sir?
   Customer: No, I didn't.
   Barber: In that case, I seem to have slipped with the razor.

A man swept into a barbershop, tossed his jacket aside, sat in a chair, and said, "Just a shave, please. I don't have time to listen to a haircut."

• *Brokers* •

Against the advice of his stockbroker, Willings bought ten thousand shares of Miraculous Mining at a dollar a share. The price doubled to two dollars.

Willings called his broker and said, "Buy ten thousand more shares." The price soared to four dollars.

Willings called again and ordered another twenty thousand shares. The price shot up to six dollars.

Willings called once again. "Time to take my profit," he said. "Sell it all."

"Sell?" his broker said. "To who?"

Fantino was legendary in the brokerage business, racking up commissions that left other brokers in awe. Not only did he have an incredible sales pitch, he also worked as many as twenty hours a day.

Eventually, it caught up with him, and he nearly collapsed from exhaustion. His company insisted that he go into the hospital for a complete checkup. Fantino complied, but all he could think of was the commissions he'd be losing while the doctors looked him over.

The nurse insisted that he lie in bed while they waited for the doctor. To keep him quiet, she put a thermometer into his mouth. Ten minutes later, she took it out and looked at it.

"Ninety-seven," she said.

Fantino was looking out the window, his mind

elsewhere. "Good," he mumbled. "When it gets to ninety-nine, sell."

Goodman was a moderately successful stockbroker who dreamed of making the big money someday. He took his friend out for a drive, and he chose the route carefully in order to impress on him the possibilities of the brokerage business.

"Look at that yacht," he said as they drove slowly past a marina. "That belongs to the senior partner at Merrill Lynch. That one over there is owned by the head of Goldman, Sachs. And look at that huge yacht out there. That's the pride and joy of the top seller at Prudential-Bache."

His friend was silent. Goodman turned to look at him and saw a pained look on his face. "What's the matter?" Goodman asked.

"I was just wondering," his friend said. "Are there any customers' yachts?"

• *Cabdrivers* •

The passenger sat in the backseat, clutching the door handle and wondering if she could expect to survive this trip. The cabdriver sped through the crowded streets, weaving in and out of traffic. The passenger watched as one pedestrian after another leapt aside to avoid being run down by her lunatic driver.

She looked ahead and saw a truck double-parked on the narrow street. Not only did the driver fail to slow down, he actually accelerated as he approached the truck. He slipped his cab through the available space with an inch or two to spare on either side.

"Driver!" the passenger screamed. "Are you trying to get us both killed?"

"Relax, lady," he said. "Just do what I do. Close your eyes."

A well-dressed businessman got into a cab in Manhattan and asked to be taken to the airport. While they were stuck in a traffic jam, the man leaned forward and spoke to the driver.

"How's your sense of adventure?" he asked.

The driver looked at him in the rearview mirror. "About as good as anyone else's," he said.

"I have a proposition for you," the man said. "I have to be in Chicago tomorrow afternoon for a meeting. The thought of flying back and forth bores me to tears. How about driving me there?"

"To Chicago?" the driver gasped.

"Sure. Why not? I'll pay for the gas and all the tolls on my expense account. We'll get there tomorrow afternoon, I'll go to my meeting and be out in an hour. I'll pay for your meals and a hotel room overnight. Then you'll drive me back. If you like, you can leave the meter running from now until we get back. What have you got to lose?"

The driver inched his cab forward into the traffic and

thought about the man's proposition. "I have nothing to lose," he said. "I'll do it."

So they took off. The cabdriver motored through New Jersey, Pennsylvania, Ohio, and Indiana and into the City of the Big Shoulders. He drove his fare to an office building and waited for his return. Then they got a couple of rooms in a hotel, had a big meal, and slept through the night. The next morning, they took off and reversed their route, arriving back in Manhattan by midday.

The meter read $4,265.90.

"I'll go into the bank and get you a certified check," the businessman said. "I'll make it for $5,000, so you'll get a sizable tip on the deal."

"Thanks," the cabdriver said, smiling.

"One other thing," the man said. "When I get the check, I'd like you to drive me home."

"Where's that?"

"Brooklyn," the man said.

"No way," the cabbie said. "Then I'd have to drive back across the bridge without a passenger."

• *Chefs* •

A Texas rancher sat in a restaurant in Chicago, shaking his head sadly as he looked down at his steak. He waved for the waiter.

"Take this thing back to the kitchen," he said. "Tell the chef to try cooking it before sending it out again."

Seconds later, the waiter returned. "Sir," he said, "the chef says that steak is cooked."

Furious, the rancher got up and stormed into the kitchen. Pointing to the offending steak, he bellowed, "You call that thing cooked?"

The chef looked at the steak, then back at him. "Yes," she said. "It's medium-rare."

"Ha!" the rancher snorted. "I've seen cows hurt worse than that who recovered!"

The customer in the Italian restaurant was so pleased that he asked to speak to the chef. The owner proudly led him into the kitchen and introduced him to the chef.

"Your veal parmigiana was superb," the customer said. "I just spent a month in Italy, and yours is better than any I ever had over there."

"Naturally," the chef said. "Over there, they use domestic cheese. Ours is imported."

• *Dentists* •

"Painless dentist, indeed! Why, he's no different from any other dentist I've been to!"

"Why, did he hurt you?"

"No, but he screamed when I bit his finger."

Dr. Morgan decided something drastic had to be done about certain patients who continually ignored his bills.

One woman owed him three thousand dollars for a set of false teeth. Fed up with waiting for his money, he drove to her house to confront her in person.

When he returned an hour later, his wife asked if had gotten his money. "No," he said angrily. "But that isn't the worst of it. She had the nerve to gnash my teeth at me."

• *Doctors* •

On a stifling hot day, a man fainted in the middle of a busy intersection. As traffic began to pile up in all directions, a woman rushed to help him. As she knelt down to loosen his collar, a man emerged from the crowd, pushed her aside, and said, "It's all right, honey. I've had a course in first aid."

She stood up and watched as he took the man's pulse and prepared to administer artificial respiration. Then she tapped him on the shoulder.

"When you get to the part about calling a doctor," she said, "I'm already here."

Patient: It isn't possible that I'm as overweight as you say I am!

Doctor: Maybe you'd prefer to look at it a different way. According to this chart, you're about ten inches too short.

. . .

"It's just a cold," the doctor said. "There is no cure, and you'll just have to live with it until it goes away."

"But Doctor," the patient whined, "it's making me so miserable."

The doctor rolled his eyes toward the ceiling. Then he said, "Look, go home and take a hot bath. Then put a bathing suit on and run around the block three or four times."

"What!" the patient exclaimed. "I'll get pneumonia!"

"We have a cure for pneumonia," the doctor said.

"I've told your aunt she needs surgery."

"What's your fee, Doctor?"

"Eight thousand dollars."

"What does my aunt have?"

"Eight thousand dollars."

"The best thing for you," the doctor said, "is to cut out all sweets and fatty foods, give up alcohol, and stop smoking."

"I see," the patient said. "To be honest, I don't deserve the best. What's second best?"

"I can't do the things I used to do," the patient said to the doctor. "I wish you had some magic way of making me younger."

"You've got it wrong," the doctor said. "My job is to see that you get older."

"Champagne, caviar, pâté de foie gras! If my doctor saw this, he'd be furious."

"Why? Does he have you on a diet?"

"No. I owe him a thousand dollars."

"If I tell you you need surgery, will you be able to afford it?"

"If I can't afford it, will you tell me I need surgery?"

"Take one of these pills after each meal," the doctor said. "And I suggest you drink an ounce of whiskey each night before you go to bed."

The patient returned two weeks later, complaining that he still did not feel well.

"Did you do what I told you to do?" the doctor asked.

"Well," the patient said, "I've fallen a little behind with the pills." Then he brightened and added, "But I'm about six months ahead with the whiskey."

Doctor: I can't do anything about your condition. I'm afraid it's hereditary.

Patient: In that case, send the bill to my parents.

. . .

"The doctor promised he'd have me walking around in a week."

"And did he?"

"He sure did. I had to sell my car to pay his bill."

• *Executives* •

Weill and Mahoney had started with only five hundred dollars between them, but they had built up a computer business with sales in the millions. Their company employed over two hundred people, and the two executives lived like princes.

Almost overnight, things changed. Sales dropped sharply, former customers disappeared, and the business failed. Weill and Mahoney blamed each other for the troubles, and they parted on unfriendly terms.

Five years later, Weill drove up to a decrepit diner and stopped for a cup of coffee. As he was wiping some crumbs from the table, a waiter approached. Weill looked up and gasped.

"Mahoney!" he said, shaking his head. "It's a terrible thing, seeing you working as a waiter in a place like this."

"Yeah," Mahoney said, curling his lip. "But *I* don't eat here."

. . .

A day in the life of a busy executive, as reflected in responses to telephone calls:

"He hasn't come in yet."

"I expect him any minute."

"He's in, but he's in conference."

"He's out to lunch."

"I expect him back any minute."

"He's somewhere in the building. His coat is here."

"He came back to the office, but now he's at a meeting."

"He's gone for the day."

"I'm going to have to fire my secretary," the executive said to his friend. "She's constantly asking me to spell the simplest words for her."

"That can be annoying," his friend said.

"Annoying, nothing!" he said. "It's embarrassing to have to say 'I don't know' all the time."

Harmon, the chief executive officer of the corporation, came back from lunch one day in a very chipper mood. He told an amusing story to some people in the clerical pool, then followed it up with two others. Within a few minutes, Harmon was surrounded by a dozen employees, all laughing loudly at his anecdotes.

During a particularly long and loud spurt of laughter, Harmon noticed that one young man, sitting away from the group, wasn't laughing. The CEO called to the young man.

"What's the matter? No sense of humor?"

"Sure I have a sense of humor," the young man said. "But I don't need to laugh. Friday's my last day."

• *Filmmakers* •

"No, no, no!" the director screamed. "Cut!" He stormed onto the set and confronted his leading man.

"That's no way to fall down a staircase!" he fumed. "What's the matter? Are you afraid of messing up your hair or getting a scratch on that pretty face of yours?"

The actor knew enough about this man's temper to keep his own mouth shut. Let the director rant for a minute or two, then they could all get back to shooting the scene.

"We can't shoot this scene if you're going to be a coward about it!" the director said. "Look, I'll show you how easy it is."

He climbed to the top of the stairs and assumed the position the actor was supposed to take. Then his body tipped toward the steps, and he tumbled to the bottom.

He looked up at the actor from the floor and said, *"Now* do you think you can do it right?"

"I guess so," the actor said.

"Good," the director said. "Everybody back into position for the shot. Oh, and by the way, somebody call an ambulance. My leg is broken."

• • •

The same director had a run-in with the stuntman who would be jumping off a cliff in place of the leading man. The stuntman checked out the spot and raced into the director's trailer.

"I absolutely refuse to make that jump," he said. There's only about a foot of water at the bottom of that cliff."

"Of course," the director said. "Do you think we want you to drown?"

• *Judges* •

The judge looked down from the bench at the man who had been arrested. The man glared back at the judge, still seething with anger at his landlord.

"So," the judge said, "you pushed your landlord down a flight of stairs."

"That's right, Your Honor," the man replied defiantly.

The judge said sternly, "You seem to think you were within your rights in doing so."

"Take a look at my lease," the man said. "I figure that anything they forgot to prohibit in that lease is something I have a right to do."

During the jury-selection process, the judge asked a prospective juror some questions.

"Have you formed any opinion about the guilt or innocence of the man on trial, Mr. Ferguson?"

"None whatsoever," Ferguson answered.

"Are you opposed to capital punishment?" the judge asked.

"Certainly not in this case."

• *Lawyers* •

Things looked bad for Mob kingpin Grossberger. The prosecution had several witnesses to the shooting, and the murder weapon had Grossberger's fingerprints all over it.

"Don't worry," his lawyer said. "I've managed to bribe one of the jurors. It'll cost you twenty grand, but he's going to hold out for a manslaughter conviction."

The jury was out for three days, but they returned with the manslaughter conviction. Grossberger got five years, and his lawyer convinced him how lucky he was to get off so lightly.

That evening, the lawyer met the juror at a prearranged spot. "You had me worried," the lawyer said. "Why did it take so long to reach a decision?"

"It wasn't easy," the juror said. "The other eleven people wanted to acquit him, but I argued them out of it."

The doctor was having lunch with a lawyer who had an office in his building. "I'm really annoyed," the doctor said. "On my way over here, I ran into someone I used to play bridge with. He kept me for ten minutes, telling me about a back pain."

"What did you do?" the lawyer asked.

"Oh, I recommended a few exercises. You know, maybe I should send him a bill. What do you think?"

"Of course you should," the lawyer said. "You gave him advice, and that's a professional service."

"You're right," the doctor said. "I'll send a bill this afternoon."

The next day, the doctor received an envelope from the lawyer. It contained a bill for two hundred dollars for legal services.

The next week, the doctor met the lawyer in the elevator. "Nice weather," the doctor said. "By the way, I really can't afford to hear your opinion of it."

"I've managed to get them to agree," the lawyer said. "It took a lot of time and energy, but I've worked out a settlement that I think is fair to both sides."

"Fair to both sides?" the client said. "I hired a lawyer for that? I could have worked that out myself!"

The lawyer listened while the prospective client explained her case. When she was finished, the lawyer stood up and smiled.

"This is an airtight case," he said. "I can't imagine a

jury ruling against you. We'll have the case wrapped up in a couple of days."

"That's awful," the woman said.

"Why?"

"Because I just gave you the other people's side."

A corporate executive received a monthly bill from the law firm that was handling a big case for his company. It included hourly billings for conferences, research, phone calls, and everything but lunch hours. Unhappy as he was, the executive knew that the company would have to pay for each of these services. Then he noticed one item buried in the middle of the list: FOR CROSSING THE STREET TO TALK TO YOU, THEN DISCOVERING IT WASN'T YOU AT ALL—$125.

The defendant was rattled by the prosecutor's driving questions and constant interruptions. "If you don't mind," he said to the prosecutor, "I'd like to tell my story in my lawyer's own words."

One lawyer said to another, "Boy, that judge makes me so mad! I really felt like telling her off again."

"What do you mean again?" his friend asked.

"I felt like it yesterday, too."

· · ·

It was a notorious insider-trading case, and the law firm of Dewey, Cheatham, and Howe put all its best people on the defense of its richest client. When the decision was finally handed down, Howe left the news on Dewey's answering machine at home.

"Justice has triumphed," Howe said.

When Dewey got the message, he called Howe's machine and left this message: "File an appeal immediately."

• *Librarians* •

An Asian exchange student had just taken out his first library card, and he read the pamphlet that explained the privileges and responsibilities that went with it.

He walked over to the information desk and said, "Excuse me, but I'm not sure I understand this pamphlet."

"Which part?" the clerk asked.

"Is it true that I can take out any record or audio tape that you have in the library?"

"That's right," the clerk said.

"And I can take out any videotape?"

"That's right."

Just then, a beautiful young librarian walked by, and the exchange student gasped.

"Can I take out any librarian?" he asked.

"Afraid not," the clerk said, smiling. "The librarians are for reference only."

· · ·

Willie had to do a book report for his seventh-grade
English class, and he asked the librarian how he should
go about choosing a book. The librarian led him to the
young adult fiction section and told him to browse.
Twenty minutes later, the librarian came back.

"Find anything?" he asked.

"Plenty of books," Willie said, "but nothing I'd care
to read."

"What's wrong with them?" the librarian asked.

"The covers are too far apart."

• *Pilots* •

"Ladies and gentlemen," the pilot said over the
loudspeaker, "may I have your attention, please. I have
some bad news and some good news."

The passengers stirred in their seats, exchanged
some worried glances, and waited for the
announcements.

"The bad news," the pilot said, "is that our engines
have failed and we're losing altitude." Then his voice
brightened. "The good news is that we're making very
good time."

An amateur pilot learned that his barber had never been
in a plane in his life. He coaxed and cajoled until he

convinced the barber to put aside his fears and come up for a flight with him.

The fears, however, accompanied the barber. All through the flight he mumbled, "What am I doing? Have I lost my mind?"

When the plane touched down, the barber hopped out and sighed with relief at being on solid ground again. He turned to the pilot and said, "Thanks for both flights."

"Both?" the puzzled pilot asked.

"My first and my last," the barber said.

O'Toole had been flying single-engine planes for years, but his mother always warned him that it was a terribly dangerous hobby. O'Toole had asked her hundreds of times to come up with him so she could find out just how safe—and exhilarating—his flights could be. Then one day, she shocked him and said she'd give it a try.

Determined to make this a memorable experience for his mother, O'Toole did everything he could to ensure she'd be comfortable. Just before takeoff, he said, "Mom, people sometimes have trouble with their ears during a flight. This should take care of any problems." He handed her a stick of gum, strapped himself into the pilot's seat, and headed for the runway.

An hour later, he touched down and taxied the plane off the runway. He helped his mother out of her seat, waiting for her report.

She stood up and smiled at him. "It was really

wonderful," she said. "But how do I get the gum out of my ears?"

An American came running up to the customs desk in Rome. Gasping for breath, she moved to the head of the line and said, "I have to make the noon plane to New York. Can you please rush me through?"

A man in the middle of the line came up to her.

"Everybody's in a hurry," he said. "But don't worry. Your plane won't leave before you get there."

She gave him an irritated look and snapped, "How the hell do you know that?"

"I'm the pilot," he said.

• *Police Officers* •

The Omaha police were searching for a man they suspected of a string of burglaries. They had six photographs of the man, all taken in different locations and from different angles. They sent fax copies of these pictures to police departments all over the country.

Three days later, Omaha received a fax report from the police chief in a small town in Iowa. The report read, "We got right to work on those six pictures you sent. We've arrested five of the suspects, and we have the sixth under observation right now."

. . .

Officer Benjamin was walking his beat when he spotted a traffic jam at a busy intersection. The east-west traffic had a green light, but the lead car wasn't moving. The light turned red, and the impatient drivers began honking. The light turned green again, but the lead car still didn't move. The honking grew louder.

Benjamin walked over to the lead car, leaned toward the window, and said to the driver, "What's the matter, friend, don't we have any colors you like?"

The chief of detectives was being interviewed at a local radio station. "Tell me," the interviewer said, "are the criminals you come across as clever as the ones we see in TV programs?"

"No," the chief said. "But then we don't work magic like the TV cops, so it all evens out in the end."

Officer Garcia spotted a double-parked car outside an office building, and she walked over to it and began writing out a summons. A man came running out of the building, shouting, "Wait! Officer, wait!"

"Is this your car?" she asked.

"Yes, it is," the man said. "But please don't write out that ticket. I have an explanation."

Continuing to write, Garcia said, "An explanation for double-parking? Let's hear it."

"I was at the dentist having a tooth pulled," the man said. "I double-parked so I'd have something to worry about to keep my mind off the pain."

. . .

The police were sure the criminal was inside the movie theater. The chief told the sergeant to surround the building and have all the exits watched.

An hour later, the sergeant returned with his men. "He got away," he told the chief.

"Got away!" the chief roared. "Did you guard all the exits like I told you?"

"Sure," the sergeant said.

"Then how did he get out?"

"Don't know. He must have used one of the entrances."

Crankshaw finished his police training and was inducted into the force. On his first day in uniform, he went to the department store where he used to work.

"Look who's here!" his former colleagues cried. *"Officer* Crankshaw."

"How do you like your new job?" one of them asked.

"Well," Crankshaw said, "the hours aren't as good as they were here. And it is dangerous. But one thing I love is that the customer is always wrong."

• *Politicians* •

Winston Churchill was once asked to name the chief qualification a politician should have. His reply: "It's the ability to foretell what will happen tomorrow, next month, and next year—and to explain afterward why it didn't happen."

Statesman: A politician who never got caught.

The senator called his chief aide in a panic. "I'm on next," he said, "and I can't find the speech I use when I abandon my prepared speech."

A newcomer to the political scene was campaigning in the backwoods for the office of assemblyman. Outside a ramshackle house, he saw a young man milking a cow. He approached the man, ready to make his pitch for a vote.

Just as he was getting started, an old man called from inside the house. "Luke, get in the house. And who is that guy you're talking to?"

"Says he's a politician, Pop," Luke said.

"In that case, you'd better bring the cow inside with you."

During the eight years he served as Eisenhower's vice president, Richard Nixon had many reminders of the esteem accorded to people in his position. Once, the Nixons were staying at a hotel in Chicago when a fire alarm went off in the middle of the night. Hundreds of guests, including Dick and Pat Nixon, were herded into the lobby. Once Nixon realized that it was a false alarm he and his wife headed for the elevator.

"Just a minute," said the hotel's security chief. "Everyone stays in the lobby until we get the all clear."

"I'm the vice president," Nixon said.

"Oh," the security chief said. "Sorry. Go right ahead."

Nixon pressed the elevator button, and the security chief had second thoughts. "Vice president?" he said. "Of what?"

"Of the United States," Nixon answered.

"Get back out here," the security chief said. "I thought you were a vice president of the hotel."

Jameson had been county sheriff for twenty years, but he always campaigned door-to-door. Running for his fifth term, he knocked on the door of one of the county's oldest residents. Mrs. Turner opened the door and reached for her umbrella, which she brandished in his direction.

"Get off my property, you slime!" she shouted.

"But Mrs. Turner," the sheriff said, "I'm here to ask for your vote in next week's election."

"Not on your life!" she said. "You're a thief, just like everyone in your family! I wouldn't vote for you if you were running against a baboon! Now get out of here!"

She slammed the door in his face, and he decided it wouldn't do to press the matter. He took a notebook

out of his pocket, flipped through the pages, and wrote
his evaluation after Mrs. Turner's name: "Doubtful."

The congressman's campaign was on the skids because
of a severe lack of funds. Things were so bad that his
fundraising dinners had been scaled back to fund-raising
speeches to save on the cost of the food.

His campaign manager called a press conference and
tried to put the best possible face on the situation. "No
more dinners," he announced. "The congressman's
supporters would rather hear him speak than eat."

"Good," one of the reporters called out. "I've already
heard him eat."

"Governor," the reporter said, "many people can't
understand from your recent speech just where you
stand on the question of air pollution."

"Good," the governor said. "It took my staff a week
to write the speech just that way."

It has been said that the United States has the best
congressmen money can buy.

"My brother worked in the mayor's campaign, hoping
to get a city job after the election."

"What's he doing now?"

"Nothing. He got the job."

. . .

A demagogue is a politician who can rock the boat and persuade everyone else that they're in a terrible storm.

A tired-looking reporter made his way out of the press conference that had been going on for over an hour. As he left the room, a woman stopped him.
    "Who's speaking in there?" she asked.
    "Senator Grimes."
    "About what?"
    "He didn't say."

A Washington reporter was awakened by her husband in the middle of the night. "I think there's a thief in the house," he said.
    "No doubt," she said sleepily. "And there are a handful in the Senate, too."

The candidate called his wife and said, "Congratulate me, I've just won the election."
    "Honestly, dear?" she said.
    "Now, why would you want to bring that up?" he grumbled.

The reporter returned to the city room from a senator's press conference. His editor asked, "What did the great statesman have to say?"

"Nothing," the reporter answered.

"Well," the editor said, "keep your report down to two thousand words."

• *Psychoanalysts* •

A man walked into a bar and ordered a glass of white wine. He took a sip of the wine, then tossed the remainder into the bartender's face.

Before the bartender could recover from the surprise, the man began weeping. "I'm sorry," he said. "I'm really sorry. I keep doing that to bartenders. I can't tell you how embarrassing it is to have a compulsion like this."

Far from being angry, the bartender was sympathetic. Before long, he was suggesting that the man see an analyst about his problem.

"I happen to have the name of a psychoanalyst," the bartender said. "My brother and my wife have both been treated by him, and they say he's as good as they come."

The man wrote down the name of the doctor, thanked the bartender, and left. The bartender smiled, knowing he'd done a good deed for a fellow human being.

Six months later, the man was back. "Did you do what I suggested?" the bartender asked, serving the glass of white wine.

"I certainly did," the man said. "I've been seeing the

psychoanalyst twice a week." He took a sip of the wine. Then he threw the remainder into the bartender's face.

The flustered bartender wiped his face with a towel. "The doctor doesn't seem to be doing you any good," he sputtered.

"On the contrary," the man said, "he's done me a world of good."

"But you threw the wine in my face again!" the bartender exclaimed.

"Yes," the man said. "But it doesn't embarrass me anymore."

Patient: Doctor, no one ever pays any attention to me.
    Doctor: Next!

"Mr. Chilton," the analyst said, "I think this will be your last visit."

"Does that mean I'm cured?" he asked.

"For all practical purposes, yes," she said. "I think we can safely say that your kleptomania is now under control. You haven't stolen anything in two years, and you seem to know where the kleptomania came from."

"Well, that's terrific, Doctor. Before I go, I'd like to tell you something. Although our relationship is strictly professional, it's been one of the most rewarding of my life. I wish I could do something to repay you for helping me."

"You've paid my fee," the doctor said. "That's the only responsibility you have."

"I know," Chilton said. "But isn't there some personal favor I could do for you?"

"Well," the doctor said, "I'll tell you what. If you ever suffer a relapse, my son could use a nice portable color television."

Analyst: Do you have trouble making up your mind?
   Patient: Well, yes and no.

"Good morning, Doctor," the man said. "I'm here because my wife insists that I need professional help."

"Why does she feel that way?" the doctor asked.

"Because I prefer bow ties to long ties."

"I don't understand," the doctor said. "Why would she see that as a problem? Many people prefer bow ties to long ties. In fact, I have the same preference myself."

"Really?" the patient said, smiling. "How do you like yours—boiled, or sautéed with a little garlic?"

Neurotic: Someone who builds castles in the air.
   Psychotic: Someone who lives in those castles.
   Psychoanalyst: The one who collects the rent.

. . .

She had been seeing the psychoanalyst for years, pouring out her heart to him twice a week. However, she was making no progress, and the doctor didn't believe she ever would.

"Mrs. Porter," he said at the end of one session, "do you think these visits are doing you any good?"

"Not really," she said. "My inferiority complex is as strong as ever."

"Mrs. Porter," the doctor said, "I have something to tell you. You don't have an inferiority complex. You are, in fact, inferior."

"Doctor, you must help us. My husband thinks he's a chicken."

"A chicken? Why don't you bring him in so I can try to cure him of this delusion?"

"I would, but we need the eggs."

• *Real Estate Agents* •

Mr. and Mrs. Ashford went to the office of a real estate agent. "We're thinking of buying a larger house," Mrs. Ashford said. "But first, we want to know how much we can get for our present house."

The agent drove home with them and looked the place over. "Let me put an ad in Sunday's paper," he said. "The response will give us an idea of how much you can sell it for."

The Ashfords agreed. The next Sunday, they read the ad that the agent had placed in the paper. Mr. Ashford immediately telephoned the agent.

"We've decided not to sell," he said.

"But why?" the agent asked.

"Your ad convinced us that this house is exactly what we want."

Walton had applied for a mortgage, and now he was appearing for his interview with the co-op board. These people had been known to turn away four out of every five prospective buyers of apartments in their building.

The head of the board said, "Now, Mr. Walton, we keep our building very quiet. Do you have any young children?"

"No, I don't."

"Do you own a piano?"

"No."

"Do you play any other musical instrument?"

"No."

"Do you have a dog, a cat, or a parrot?"

"No," Walton said, getting exasperated. "But I think I should warn you that I file my nails about once every two weeks."

The houses in the new development were cheap, but it was clear that the builder hadn't used the best materials. The agent led a prospective buyer into one of the houses.

"Wait here," she said. "I'm going into the next room."

The customer stayed put. Then he heard her call his name. "Can you hear me?"

"Just barely," the customer said.

"Can you see me?"

"Of course not."

Returning to the room, the agent said, "Pretty impressive walls, wouldn't you say?"

A man walked into a real estate agent's office and said, "I'm moving from that apartment you rented me last year. Do you know where I can buy a couple of hundred cockroaches?"

"Of course not," the agent said. "Why would you want to buy cockroaches?"

"The lease says the apartment has to be in the same condition as when I moved in."

• *Undertakers* •

"Good afternoon," Carrington said into the phone. "Carrington Funeral Home."

"Mr. Carrington," the voice on the phone said, "this is John Gustav. I need you to make arrangements for the burial of my wife."

"Your wife!" Carrington gasped. "But Mr. Gustav, I buried your wife two years ago!"

"Yes," Gustav said sadly. "I recently remarried."
"Well, congratulations!"

Minutes before the cremation, the undertaker quietly sat down next to the grieving widow. "How old was your husband?" he asked.

"He was ninety-eight," she answered softly. "Two years older than I am."

"Really?" the undertaker said. "Hardly worth going home, wouldn't you say?"

On doctor's orders, Melling had moved to Arizona. Two weeks later, he was dead. His body was shipped back home, where the undertaker prepared it for the services.

Melling's brother came in to make sure everything was taken care of. "Would you like to see the body?" the undertaker asked.

"I might as well take a look at it before the others get here."

The undertaker led him into the next room and opened the top half of the casket. He stood back and proudly displayed his work.

"He looks good," the brother said. "Those two weeks in Arizona were just the thing for him."

■ ■ ■

Mostly True Stories About Mostly Famous People

▲

Here you'll find anecdotes about people your listeners are likely to recognize: actors, writers, politicians, and folks who are famous for nothing more than being famous—celebrities.

We've called them "mostly true stories" because some of them are a bit hard to verify. If some stories are less than absolutely factual, however, you have this consolation: they all sound as if they should *be true.*

▼

Johnny Carson, the quintessential talk-show host of the twentieth century, is a man with a deep distrust of the press. Every now and then, however, he has been known to loosen up and give hungry reporters something to report.

That's what he did while visiting Harvard to receive an award. It was one of the rare times that Carson subjected himself to the sometimes inane questions of the press, and he maintained his cool demeanor throughout.

One desperate reporter asked, "What would you like to have inscribed on your tombstone?"

"I'll be right back," Carson quipped.

William Marcy Tweed—Boss Tweed to everyone who knew his name—was the head of Tammany Hall, the most powerful political machine in the history of New York City, and probably of the country. Tweed bragged openly about the power he bought with huge bribes. He once claimed to have spent $600,000 to get the state legislature to adopt a new city charter that gave him even more power than he'd had before. He scoffed at reformers, who couldn't touch his organization, no matter how much noise they made. "As long as I count the votes," he said to one do-gooder, "what are you going to do about it?"

Tweed treated the press with the same contempt, telling them to publish all the exposés they could get their hands on. But one activity of the press did concern him. Tweed was infuriated by the caricatures of him that artist Thomas Nast supplied to *Harper's Weekly*. "My constituents can't read," he said, "but they can see pictures!"

Eventually, Tweed was arrested, charged, and convicted of bribery, then sentenced to serve twelve years in prison. His influence was so great, however, that he was allowed to visit his home every day. One day, he simply slipped away.

He took off for Spain, where he was sure he'd be safe from the prying eyes of the press. Within months, he was identified, arrested, and brought back to serve his time. His downfall? Someone in Spain had recognized him from one of Nast's caricatures.

Humorist Robert Benchley, while visiting Venice, sent a telegram to actor David Niven. The telegram read: STREETS FILLED WITH WATER. PLEASE ADVISE.

Charles Chaplin, Jr., liked to tell about the time his father attended a contest to see who could do the best Chaplin imitation. Dozens of contestants, all wearing the battered black hat and baggy suit and carrying the trademark cane, got up and did their best to simulate the famous walk and two or three of the movements that had made Chaplin known throughout the world. Without identifying himself, Chaplin got up on the stage and did the routine.

He came in third.

Playwright George S. Kaufman was once unfortunate enough to be sitting in front of a nonstop talker at the theater. The moment she took her seat, the woman began holding forth on the décor of the theater, the appearance of certain members of the audience, the high price of tickets, and everything else that came to mind. During the first act, she passed judgment on the dialogue, the set, and the talents of the actors, all loudly enough for everyone in the vicinity to hear.

As the curtain fell and the house lights went up, she told her companion how much she hated standing in the lobby during intermission and how she was equally displeased at the prospect of sitting in her seat without the chance to stretch her legs.

Kaufman turned in his seat and frowned at her. "Madame," he said, "do you never have an *unexpressed* thought?"

In the late nineteenth century, a bishop of the United Brethren church was discussing philosophy with a college professor. The bishop's opinion was that the millennium was at hand. As evidence, he cited the facts that everything about nature had already been discovered and that all useful inventions had already been made.

As the story goes, the professor politely told the bishop that he was mistaken. "Why, in a few years," he said, "we'll be able to fly through the air."

"What a nonsensical idea," the bishop said. "Flight," he assured the professor, "is reserved for the birds and the angels."

Bishop Wright was the father of two young budding inventors named Orville and Wilbur.

It is generally conceded that George Gershwin was a musical genius, and no one was more convinced of this than George himself. He once attended a concert featuring a pianist from Spain. When the concert was over, Gershwin's friend said, "Isn't he great, George?"

"He's a genius," Gershwin said. "A Spanish Gershwin."

Pianist Oscar Levant, a well-known wit and a good friend of George Gershwin, once asked the composer, "If you had it to do all over, George, would you fall in love with yourself again?"

While we're on the subject of musical geniuses, there's a story about violinist Fritz Kreisler. He was once asked by a very rich woman how much he would charge to perform at a private party. Kreisler said his fee would be five thousand dollars. The woman's eyebrows shot up, but she agreed to the amount.

"Please remember," she added haughtily, "that I do not expect you to mingle with my guests."

"In that case," Kreisler said, "my fee will be only four thousand dollars."

Edmund Kean (1787–1833) was considered by many to be the greatest Shakespearean actor of his time. His first dramatic success was in the role of Shylock in *The Merchant of Venice,* and he later played virtually every one of Shakespeare's leading characters. He was the consummate actor, and he was probably responsible for more than one of our stereotypes of nineteenth-century stage performers.

There is a legend about Kean's last moments on earth. As he lay dying, his son approached the bed. The young man leaned over, wiped his father's brow, and asked, "Is it difficult for you, Father?"

"No," Kean said. "Dying is easy." Then he added, *"Comedy* is hard."

Winston Churchill once had a private secretary who believed that the prime minister needed constant instruction in English grammar. The secretary was particularly obsessed with prepositions and with Churchill's tendency to use them at the ends of sentences.

Letters and memoranda, drafts of speeches and notes to friends would all come back from the secretary with notations about this failing. The secretary was determined to break his boss of the nasty grammatical habit.

One day, Churchill received a draft with at least a dozen corrections. Every one of them pointed out a sentence that ended with a preposition. Exasperated, Churchill scrawled a note to his secretary, hoping to break *him* of his annoying habit. He clipped the note to the document.

The note read: "This is the kind of thing up with which I will not put!"

Calvin Coolidge was known as Silent Cal because of his unwillingness to speak unless it was absolutely necessary. His critics also thought that he was a president who did as little as possible, preferring to let the country run itself.

When writer Dorothy Parker was told that Coolidge had just died, she responded, "How can they tell?"

Coolidge's stinginess with words was even evident during his campaigns. At the time he was running for office, the most common method of reaching the people was the whistle-stop train. At one such stop, Coolidge stepped out to the rear of the railroad car and looked the crowd over. Then he calmly stepped back inside.

"What's the matter?" his campaign manager asked.

"This crowd," he said, "is too big for an anecdote and too small for an oration."

Press agents and other publicity people are under constant pressure to invent ways to get their clients noticed by the public. Back in the 1940s, one Hollywood press agent manufactured an event that got his clients—comics Bud Abbott and Lou Costello—into newspapers across the country.

The agent persuaded them to take out a unique policy with Lloyd's of London. Lloyd's had long been known for a willingness to insure just about anything, as long as the client was willing to pay the premium.

The Abbott and Costello policy promised to pay $100,000 to the survivors of anyone who died laughing during one of their performances.

It was just another Cecil B. DeMille epic—a biblical movie with a cast of thousands, a crew of several hundred, and a legendary director who insisted on perfection from everyone on the set. Even for a DeMille spectacular, though, it had been a particularly trying day.

Normally, movies are filmed in tiny pieces, so tiny that actors often have no sense of what an entire scene will look like. Because of production demands, however, this day's scene was going to be shot live, with all six hundred or so actors and extras going into action at once.

DeMille had stationed eleven cameras at various points; six to pick up the overall action from different angles, and five to film plot developments involving the major characters. The scene had been rehearsed four times since they had started at six in the morning. After each rehearsal, hundreds of actors and dozens of technicians would go back to square one to get ready to begin again.

Now it was late afternoon. The sun was on its way down behind the hills, and there was just time enough to get the shot itself done. DeMille looked over the panorama, saw that all was right, and gave the command for action.

One hundred extras stormed down a hill. Another hundred stormed up the same hill, ready to do mock battle. In another location, fifty Roman centurions lashed at two hundred slaves who labored to move a huge stone monument toward its resting place.

Meanwhile, the principal characters acted out, in close-up, their reactions to the battle on the hill. Their words were drowned out by the noises around them, but the dialogue would be dubbed in later.

The scene took a good fifteen minutes to complete. When it was over, DeMille yelled, "Cut!" and turned to his assistant director. "I thought it was terrific!" DeMille said smiling.

"It was, C. B.," the assistant said excitedly. "It went off perfectly."

Enormously pleased, the director turned to face the head of his camera crew to find out if all the cameras had picked up what they were assigned to film. He waved to the camera supervisor.

From the top of a hill, the camera supervisor waved back. Then he called out, "Ready when you are, C. B.!"

At the height of his fame, the world-famous tenor Enrico Caruso was accustomed to being treated like visiting royalty wherever he went. On April 18, 1906, Caruso was unfortunate enough to be in San Francisco, getting ready to give a performance. He thus lived through one of the most destructive earthquakes in American history.

Having lived through the disaster, however, wasn't sufficient for the temperamental Caruso. He denounced the city of San Francisco and swore that he'd never return to a city "where disorders like that are permitted."

As an eminent politician, Britain's prime minister Margaret Thatcher has had to deal with the usual brickbats about femininity being at odds with most forms of worldly success. As her husband, businessman Denis Thatcher has found it helpful to exhibit a sense of humor when dealing with the nasty insinuations of the press. One reporter asked the tiresome question, "Who wears the pants in your family?"

"I do," Denis Thatcher replied. Then, after a pause, he added, "I also wash and iron them."

. . .

Back in the nineteenth century, Susan B. Anthony, the tireless fighter for women's rights, had a problem similar to Mrs. Thatcher's—a constant difficulty in being taken seriously by men. She was once confronted by Samuel May, a well-known abolitionist.

"You are not married," May said to her. "You have no business discussing marriage."

Holding her temper, Anthony replied, "And you are not a slave, Mr. May. What business do you have lecturing on slavery?"

Susan B. Anthony called on editor Horace Greeley one day in 1860 to ask for his newspaper's support for women's suffrage. Greeley was not sympathetic. He was an opponent of women's rights, mainly because he considered women to be of no military value.

"What would you do," he asked, "in the event of a civil war?"

"I would do just what you would do," Anthony replied. "I would sit in my office and write articles urging other people to go and fight."

Voltaire was highly regarded by many people in his own country, but to most people in England, he was just another Frenchman. When he visited London in 1727, he actually had good reason to fear for his life.

Walking along a street one day, he found himself

facing an angry crowd of people. Calls of "Hang the Frenchman!" came from the throng.

Voltaire, however, was too quick to be outwitted by an unruly mob. Taking a couple of steps backward, he called out, "Englishmen! You want to kill me because I am a Frenchman? Am I not already punished enough in not being an Englishman?"

The crowd not only applauded, they saw to it that Voltaire got home safely.

Even more than the average citizen, comedian W. C. Fields was easily annoyed by a persistent salesman. One insurance salesman refused to be shaken, even following Fields into the barbershop. The salesman just kept babbling through his various pitches, hoping eventually to wear down Fields's resistance.

Finally, Fields had had enough. "How many times do I have to say no to you?" he bellowed, spraying shaving cream all over the floor. "Just to get rid of you, I'll talk to my lawyer about it in the morning."

Still not satisfied, the salesman asked, "And will you do the right thing if he likes my offer?"

"I certainly will!" Fields shouted. "I'll get a new lawyer!"

When Stephen Douglas was a young man, he made a reputation for himself by debating political issues all over the state of Illinois. More often than not, he would spot a tall, lanky younger man sitting up front listening carefully, watching his every move, and frantically taking notes on everything Douglas said and did.

After months of this, Douglas confronted the younger man. "Why do I see you at so many of my debates?" he asked. "And what are those notes you're always scribbling?"

"I come to your debates," the young man said, "because I hope to be a debater myself someday. I take notes because I want to be at least as good as you are."

"Wonderful!" Douglas said, clapping the lad on the back. "What's your name, young man?"

"My name is Abe."

"Abe what?" Douglas asked.

"Abe Grossman."

◆ *All right, so it isn't a true story. It's funny, isn't it?*

Author James Michener was once invited by President Eisenhower to a dinner at the White House. He wrote a letter to Eisenhower explaining why he couldn't accept.

> I received your invitation three days after I had agreed to speak a few words at a dinner honoring the wonderful high school teacher who taught me how to write. I know you will not miss me at your dinner, but she might at hers.

In his lifetime, a man lives under fifteen or sixteen presidents, but a really fine teacher comes into his life but rarely.

Eisenhower wrote back to say that he understood.

Willie Sutton, one of the most famous bank robbers of the twentieth century, was the subject of numerous books, a TV drama, and at least one song. He was also a favorite of newspaper reporters, who could count on him for the kind of quote that makes a headline bounce.

Sutton had spent most of his adult life in prison. Though he escaped more than once, his short bursts of freedom always ended with an arrest for bank robbery. In an attempt to learn why he continued along such a futile course, one reporter asked, "Willie, why do you keep robbing banks?"

"Because," Sutton said smoothly, "that's where the money is."

Aside from being a playwright, George Ade (1866–1944) was also well known as a humorist on the traveling lecture circuit. Ade, Mark Twain, and others on this circuit became the earliest stand-up comedians.

One after-dinner speech of Ade's had his audience rocking with laughter. After Ade sat down to tumultuous applause, a locally famous lawyer rose to speak. He had probably had a little too much to drink, and he rolled up to the lectern with his hands in his pants pockets.

"Doesn't it strike the company as unusual," the lawyer bellowed, "that a professional humorist should actually be funny?"

When the polite laughter died down, Ade stood next to the would-be wit. "Doesn't it strike the company as unusual," Ade said, "that a lawyer should have his hands in his own pockets?"

During the Republican National Convention of 1912, the party anticipated heavy press coverage of the speech to be delivered by Theodore Roosevelt in his attempt to be elected to a third term. The Republicans had arranged for three million copies of the speech to be distributed. At the next-to-last minute, the publisher of the speech learned that no one had secured permission to use the photographs of Roosevelt and his running mate, Hiram Johnson, that would be printed as part of the speech. Under the existing copyright laws, it would have cost the publisher a dollar a copy to run the photos without permission.

The printing had already been paid for, and Roosevelt's campaign manager was not about to let three million copies of the speech be burned as scrap. So he sent a telegram to the Chicago studio that owned the rights to the pictures:

Planning to issue three million copies Roosevelt speech with pictures of Roosevelt and Johnson on cover. Great publicity opportunity for photographers. What will you pay us to use your photographs?

Within an hour, he had a telegram in reply:

Appreciate opportunity, but can only pay $250.

Will Hays (1879–1954) was a Republican politician who was appointed by the movie industry to serve as their arbiter of good taste. Although he held the office from 1921 until 1945, it was during the middle and late 1930s that the Hays Office had its strongest effect on the content of American movies, watching carefully to see that films did not let crime, immorality, or divorce go unpunished.

When Hays was first appointed to oversee the morals of Hollywood's moviemakers, his office issued a list of twelve don'ts for them to follow. The show business newspaper *Variety* headlined their story on this list, "Hays Two Up on Moses!"

Nostalgia often causes people to "remember" things about the good old days that never really happened. However, in some ways, things really were a lot simpler back then. In 1929, for example, President Herbert Hoover waited until he'd been in office forty days before calling in his secretary of war. Hoover asked the secretary, "Do you know of anything particular going on in your sphere about which I should be informed?"

"Not a thing in the world, Mr. President," the secretary answered.

And that was the last time the president and his secretary of war had occasion to get together.

Huey Long, the Louisiana politician who had hopes of running for the presidency in 1936, began as an unschooled farm boy and ended up in the governor's mansion, one of the most popular politicians in the history of the state. Long was born in the central part of Louisiana, and when he first campaigned for governor, he was given some advice about the voters in the New Orleans area.

"South Louisiana is different from the northern part of the state," he was told. "We have a lot of Catholic voters down here."

Long nodded knowingly and went out to make his speech. It began, "When I was a boy, I'd get up at six every Sunday morning, hitch our old horse up to the buggy, and take my Catholic grandparents to mass. I'd bring them home and then take my Baptist grandparents to church."

The speech was a rousing success. Afterward, a New Orleans political boss said, "Huey, you've been holding out on us. We didn't know you had Catholic grandparents."

Huey looked at him slyly and said, "We didn't even have a horse."

. . .

Francis Bacon, one of the perennial favorites as the man who *really* wrote the plays attributed to William Shakespeare, was not only an accomplished essayist, but a philosopher, scientist, and lawyer as well. He reached the peak of the legal profession when he was appointed Lord Chancellor in 1618.

In one case over which Bacon presided, the defendant was a man named Hogg. The man half-jokingly argued that he should be acquitted of the charges against him because of his relationship to the judge.

"Hogg," he said, "must be kin to Bacon."

"Not until it has been hung," the Lord Chancellor replied.

Late in her life, actress Ethel Barrymore invited a group of friends to celebrate her birthday with her. "Will there be a birthday cake?" one friend asked.

"Of course," she said. "There will be plenty of cake for everyone."

"And candles?" another friend asked.

"No," Barrymore said. "It will be a birthday party, not a torchlight procession."

In 1916, Ethel Barrymore's brother John appeared in his first Broadway success, and he decided that he should live the life of a prominent actor. He rented an apartment in New York City and spent a good deal of his earnings furnishing it.

Barrymore concluded that a garden on the roof of the building was just the thing he needed to proclaim to the world how important he really was. He had several tons of soil carted up to the roof and laid out in preparation.

It didn't take long for the owner of the building to find out what Barrymore had done. He stormed into the actor's apartment and roared, "The roof can't hold that kind of weight! It might collapse any minute!"

"Are you sure?" Barrymore asked.

"Of course I'm sure!" the landlord bellowed. "Now, what are you going to do about it?"

Barrymore shrugged his shoulders and said, "I'll move. You don't expect me to live in an unsafe building, do you?"

Thomas Edison was not only the most prolific inventor of all time, but also a careful man with a dollar. During one period of his life, he encouraged guests at his summer home to tour the grounds and inspect the various inventions he had laid out for display. To enter his garden, each visitor had to pass through a turnstile, which required a good bit of strength to push.

"Why do you have this thing here?" a guest asked. "It seems like nothing but an annoyance."

Edison smiled at his guest's naïveté. "Every single soul who pushes his way through that turnstile," he explained, "pumps seven gallons of water into the tank on my roof."

. . .

Remember the trouble you used to have with book reports in elementary school—then in junior high and high school? Somehow, it always seemed to be a question of getting started. If you could only get the ball rolling, the paper would more or less write itself.

Budd Schulberg, author of such classics as *What Makes Sammy Run?* and *The Harder They Fall,* is one professional writer who never progressed much beyond those book-report days. He once explained his writing technique to an interviewer.

"First I clean the typewriter. Then I go through my shelves and return all borrowed books. Then I play with my three children. Then, if it's warm, I go for a swim. Then I find some friends to have a drink with. By then, it's time to clean the typewriter again."

Budd Schulberg's elaborate procrastination might have won some polite applause from O. Henry, who was once responsible for churning out a short story every week for the *New York World.* Although he wrote more than 200 short stories, O. Henry had a great deal of trouble meeting his deadlines.

When asked by an editor if he had written a story that was overdue, O. Henry would almost invariably reply that he had. When the editor asked for the story, O. Henry would point to his head.

The story was written, all right. It just wasn't on paper yet.

. . .

Maybe one of the things that keeps writers from actually writing is a fear of having their work rejected. On the other hand, some writers have actually made a collection of the rejection slips they've received.

Playwright Russel Crouse once told a group of writers about the most interesting rejection slip he'd ever heard of. It said, "I am returning this paper. Someone wrote on it." It was signed by the editor.

Michael Arlen, author of *The Green Hat* and *The Flying Dutchman,* was in New York City in 1944, during a low point in his career. In an attempt to cheer himself up, he went to have dinner at a restaurant known for its celebrity clientele and cheerful atmosphere.

As he was walking into the restaurant, he met movie producer Sam Goldwyn. Arlen tried to steer the conversation in a direction that would allow him to ask Goldwyn for a job, but Goldwyn, as usual, was holding court rather than conversing. The producer offered some advice about buying racehorses as an investment, then went into the restaurant.

At the bar, Arlen met Louis B. Mayer, perhaps Goldwyn's most hostile competitor and a man Arlen had known for years. Mayer asked him what he planned to do in the near future.

"Well," Arlen said, "I was just talking to Sam Goldwyn—"

"What did he offer you?" Mayer said quickly.

Thinking of the useless advice Goldwyn had given him, Arlen answered, "Not enough, really."

Mayer grabbed his arm and said, "Would you take fifteen thousand for thirty weeks?"

The low point in Arlen's career was a thing of the past.

Ludwig van Beethoven had just finished performing one of his own compositions, and he was surrounded by a crowd of admirers. Each person tried to outdo the others in praising both the work and the performance.

"If only God had given me such a gift of genius," one woman gushed.

Beethoven turned an unfriendly look on her. "It isn't genius, madam," he said coldly. "It isn't magic either. You can be as good as I am. All you have to do is practice on your piano eight hours a day for forty years."

Pablo Picasso sat at an outdoor café in Paris, enjoying a drink with an American soldier. When Picasso explained the kind of art he was known for, the soldier shook his head.

"Sorry, but I don't like modern art," he said.

"Why not?" Picasso asked.

"Modern paintings aren't realistic," the soldier said. "I like paintings that look just like the things they're paintings of."

Picasso didn't react to this comment. Instead, he

waited until the soldier offered to show him some
pictures of his girlfriend back home. Picasso took one
of the pictures and looked at it for several seconds.

"My goodness," he said, "is she really this small?"

Early movie audiences seemed to have a related
problem with realism. When director D. W. Griffith
"invented" the close-up shot, the first reactions weren't
very encouraging. Looking at the actors on the screen,
perplexed members of the audience often asked,
"Where are their feet?"

On a visit to Scotland, General Ulysses S. Grant was
treated to a demonstration of a game he'd never heard
of before, something called golf. His host wanted to
show Grant how the game was played, even though he
wasn't much of a golfer himself.

While Grant watched, the man placed a ball on a tee,
stood back, and took a swing. Although he missed the
ball, he did tear up a patch of grass. He tried again,
with the same result. Again and again he sent patches
of dirt and grass into the air without once hitting the
ball.

Grant looked from his perspiring host to the ball,
then back to his host. "There seems to be a fair
amount of exercise in the game," he said, "but I fail to
see the purpose of the ball."

• • •

Comedian Fred Allen began his career as a vaudeville performer in theaters near his home in Boston. Before he realized how good he was at making people laugh, he presented himself as a juggler. (He later referred to his routine as the world's worst juggling act.)

From the seats and from the wings, he had seen many an act greeted with deadly silence. Terrified by the possibility that his act would suffer the same fate, Allen came onstage with a large card bearing a message for the audience. The message: "Mr. Allen is quite deaf. If you care to applaud, please do so loudly."

Fred Allen was unmatched in his skill at ludicrous exaggeration. For example, he's the creator of the often-quoted line, "My hotel room was so small, the mice were hunchbacked." He once wrote to a friend that the country spot where he was vacationing was so quiet, "I was jolted by the sound of a caterpillar backing into a globule of dew." Of his stay at a farm, he wrote, "The mosquitoes in these parts are enormous. One stung a Greyhound bus the other night and it swelled up so badly they couldn't get it through the Lincoln Tunnel."

Margot Asquith (1864–1945), wife of the British prime minister Lord Herbert Henry Asquith, was famous for her quick wit and sharp tongue.

When she and movie star Jean Harlow met for the first time, Harlow was careless enough to address the lady by her first name. To make matters worse, Harlow pronounced the name as though it rhymed with "lot."

Lady Asquith drew herself up to her full height and corrected Harlow by saying, "My dear, the *t* is silent, as in 'Harlow.' "

Author Erma Bombeck is one of those women who are constantly explaining to the world how a woman who makes more money than her husband doesn't have to spend all her time soothing his hurt feelings. As a public-school principal, William Bombeck made only a fraction of what his famous wife earned for her columns and books.

Erma Bombeck's explanation is simple. "I am overpaid and he is underpaid," she once said. "I equate it with calling in a baby-sitter. You're saying, 'I'm entrusting you now with my children. I went through twenty-six hours of labor with this kid, I have put $56,000 worth of vitamins in him, and now I'll pay you fifty cents an hour.' It doesn't make sense. If it's such a precious commodity to you, then why are you trusting it to a sophomore in tennis shoes?"

Clarence Darrow, the lawyer who built a reputation for defending highly unpopular causes, almost never asked about ability to pay before deciding to take a case. As a result, he often found that his clients had no way of paying him for his legal services.

After one of his cases had come to a happy

conclusion, his client said gleefully, "How can I ever show my appreciation, Mr. Darrow?"

Darrow replied drily, "Ever since the Phoenicians invented money, there has been only one answer to that question."

Financier J. P. Morgan could deftly manipulate the press to generate business publicity, but he believed in keeping his private life as sheltered as possible. He also expected everyone who worked for him to have the same attitude about their own privacy.

When an assistant of his made headlines for his capers with a chorus girl, Morgan called the man into his office. "You're a great disappointment to me," Morgan said.

"Why, Mr. Morgan?" the young man said. "At least I'm not a hypocrite. I haven't done anything that others don't do behind closed doors."

"You fool!" Morgan said. "What do you think doors are for?"

As the editor of a small-town newspaper, Mark Twain had to deal with many problems that would hardly qualify as journalistic. He once received a letter from a subscriber who said he had found a spider inside his newspaper and wanted to know if it signified good or bad luck.

Twain's response: "Finding a spider in your paper was neither good luck nor bad luck for you. The spider was merely looking over our paper to see which merchant is not advertising so that he can go to that store, spin his web across the door, and lead a life of undisturbed peace ever afterward."

Long before he became a candidate for the presidency, Adlai Stevenson owned a grand house near Lake Forest, Illinois. Shortly after he and his family moved in, the house was destroyed by fire. While Stevenson watched his house go up in flames, a piece of smoldering wood landed near his feet. He picked the wood up and used it to light his cigarette.

Then he turned to the fire chief and said, "At least I'm still getting some use out of the house."

Playwright-critic George Bernard Shaw once led a visitor on a tour of his home. The visitor was surprised to see no flowers on display.

"Not a single vase of flowers in the house," he said. "I thought you loved flowers."

"I do," Shaw said. "I love children, too. But I don't cut off their heads and stick them in pots to decorate my house."

At a dinner party, Shaw was pestered by the nonstop talker sitting next to him. Near the end of the meal, Shaw said to the man, "You know, between the two of us, we know everything there is to be known."

"Really?" the man said. "Why do you say that?"

Shaw replied, "You seem to know everything except that you're a bore. And I know that."

Writer Gertrude Stein was, if nothing else, a master at generating publicity for herself. During her tour of the United States in 1931, reporters who showed up at her press conferences and staged events usually had in mind some sarcastic little piece that might serve as a filler for a back page of the newspaper. More often than not, they ended up giving her front-page coverage. The woman who coined the name "Lost Generation" for the expatriate Americans who tooled around Europe after World War I was also responsible for an expression that would later be used to characterize places all over the United States. When asked by a reporter to give her impressions of Oakland, California, she replied, "There's no *there* there."

Steel magnate Andrew Carnegie, the well-known philanthropist, kept a close eye on just where each of his contributions went.

He was once approached by the secretary of the New York Philharmonic Society for a contribution of $60,000, which would allow the group to pay off some of its debts. At first, Carnegie agreed. Then he abruptly changed his mind. "There must be other people," he said, "who like music enough to help with their own money."

He told the secretary to find someone else who would contribute $30,000. If the secretary was successful, Carnegie would match the contribution.

The next day, the secretary returned, happily announcing that he'd found another donor. Pleased, Carnegie wrote out a check for $30,000. Then he said, "Would you mind telling me who gave you the other half?"

"Mrs. Carnegie," the secretary said.

Art Buchwald, who has been roasting Washington politicians and bureaucrats for decades, began writing political satire during the Eisenhower administration. The first time his good-natured joking raised some hackles was in 1957, when Eisenhower's press secretary James Hagerty took offense at one of Buchwald's columns.

Firing arrows at Hagerty's habit of reporting on the tiniest details of Eisenhower's activities, the column was a series of questions and answers about what the president said and did as he prepared to go to bed the night before.

Hagerty was infuriated by the spoof, and his public comments on it gave an enormous boost to Buchwald's growing reputation. Eisenhower put a stop to the comments by revealing that he found the column amusing.

Before the president stepped into the fray, however, Hagerty had already gone public with the charge that Buchwald was a writer of "unadulterated rot." When asked by reporters to comment on this, Buchwald replied that he wrote only adulterated rot.

When Albert Einstein accepted an invitation to join the faculty at Princeton University, his arrival caused a great stir among the national press. He received the full celebrity treatment, right down to inane questions about such things as his opinion of American women and how he had chosen a name for his cat.

Einstein was invariably pleasant to the press and public alike, but he never seemed to understand why people treated him as anything more than a physics professor. His modesty is nicely illustrated by the story of the young girl who stopped in to see him every day on her way home from school.

One day, the girl's mother met Einstein and asked, "What do you two talk about every day?"

"She brings me cookies," Einstein laughed, "and I help her with her arithmetic homework."

P. T. Barnum, who dedicated his life to entertaining the masses while he hoodwinked them, often relied on inflated language to sell his sometimes less-than-noteworthy attractions. His posters and announcements were peppered with words like *mammoth, extraordinary, colossal,* and *gargantuan.*

In one of his museums, Barnum found that he was having trouble getting the crowds to leave once they'd seen all the attractions, and it was cutting into his profits. So he devised a way of tricking the customers into walking out of the building. He posted a huge sign, elaborately lettered to draw as much attention as possible, that read THIS WAY TO THE EGRESS.

Most of his patrons expected to see some bizarre animal that Barnum had retrieved from one of the far corners of the earth. All P. T. had promised them, however, was the exit.

Jack Benny and George Burns became friends when both were young performers working their way up through the vaudeville circuit, and they remained friends until Benny died. One day, they were lunching at a Hollywood restaurant, and Benny was wrestling with the problem of whether or not to butter his bread.

"I like butter on my bread," he said. "But my diet strictly forbids butter. Maybe I should call Mary and ask her what to do."

"Jack," Burns said, "don't be ridiculous. You're a grown man. You should be able to decide, without your wife's help, whether or not to butter your own bread."

"You're right," Benny said. "I'll just have the butter, that's all."

When the waiter arrived with the check, Burns pointed to Benny and said, "He's paying."

"What?" Benny said. "Why should I have to pay the whole bill?"

"Because if you don't," Burns said, "I'll tell Mary about the butter."

. . .

That was the same Jack Benny who, when accepting a
plaque for his charity work, said, "I really don't deserve
this award. However, I have arthritis, and I don't
deserve that either."

Once Marie Curie became famous as the discoverer of
radium, she was plagued by autograph hounds. After
putting up with them for years, she finally decided not
to give another autograph under any circumstance.
    One autograph collector, knowing about her decision,
sent her a personal check for twenty-five dollars with
instructions for her to donate the amount to any charity
she chose. He figured the endorsed check would be a
nice addition to his collection of rare autographs.
    Curie, however, saw through his scheme, and she
had her secretary send him the following note:

> Madame Curie has asked me to thank you most
> kindly for your check, which, however, she is not
> going to cash. It so happens that she is an
> autograph collector and therefore will add your
> signature to her collection.

William F. Buckley carefully nurtures his public persona
as an imperious, condescending, vitriolic critic of
everyone of whom he disapproves. One question often

asked is whether this persona has any basis in reality. Decide for yourself.

While Buckley was still in elementary school, he wrote a letter to King George V of England excoriating him for not having paid Great Britain's war debt to the United States. At the British prep school he attended, he recited a list of the school's shortcomings to the president of the school. At another prep school, he crashed a faculty meeting to tell the teachers how they might do a better job than they had been doing. Years later, he did much the same thing at a faculty meeting at Yale.

He has rarely been tempted to suppress criticism since.

In the caustic critic category, journalist Heywood Broun deserves some mention. Although most of the people who knew Broun loved him, he could be merciless in his writing, especially in his drama criticism.

One Broadway performance led him to write in his review that Geoffrey Steyne was the worst actor on the American stage. Steyne decided to sue him for that remark.

The suit generated a lot of publicity, touching as it did on such topics as freedom of the press and the nature of criticism in the arts. Eventually, the suit was thrown out of court, but people in the theater community did not forget it.

Not long afterward, Steyne appeared in a new play, and Broun was sent to review it. A lot of people were eager to see if Broun's review would reflect his recent brush with the libel laws. In his review the next morning, Broun didn't mention the actor until the closing sentence, which read, "Mr. Steyne's performance was not up to his usual standard."

Artist James McNeill Whistler was never one to let his income determine his level of spending. As a result, he spent a lot of his time fending off creditors. No matter how little intention he had of paying them, however, he was always courteous to those who dunned him.

One creditor showed up at Whistler's home in an attempt to extract payment. Whistler offered him a glass of champagne.

The offer made the creditor visibly angry. "If you can't afford to pay my bill," he spouted, "how can you afford champagne?"

Whistler asked him to calm down. Then he explained, "I assure you, I haven't paid for the champagne either."

Actor James Cagney's wife often commented on her husband's phenomenal memory. In one story she told, she and Cagney were getting into a car in New York City when he spotted a man across the street. Cagney pointed him out and said, "His name is Nathan Skidelsky. He sat next to me in school."

Mrs. Cagney was doubtful. Prodigious memory or not, she couldn't believe that her husband could identify someone he hadn't seen for decades. So she challenged him to prove that his claim was true. Cagney accepted the challenge, crossed the street, and talked with the man.

"And you know what?" Mrs. Cagney said. "It *was* Nathan Skidelsky. The only problem was, he didn't remember who Jimmy Cagney was."

When essayist Charles Lamb was a boy, his father used to take him to the cemetery to visit his mother's grave. During one such visit, Charles began reading the inscriptions on the various tombstones. After he'd read a sizable number, he turned to his father.

"Where," he asked, "do they bury all the bad people?"

British poet W. H. Auden was once hired to give a series of lectures at the New School in New York's Greenwich Village. When he arrived for his first lecture, he saw that the entire auditorium was filled. Apologizing in advance for what he thought might be a less-than-stentorian delivery, he said, "If there are any of you who do not hear me, please don't raise your hands because I am also nearsighted."

After a half-century in the newspaper business, Arthur Brisbane was offered a six-month vacation—with full pay—by his employer William Randolph Hearst. When

Brisbane turned the offer down, Hearst asked for an explanation.

"There are two reasons," Brisbane said. "The first is that it might affect the circulation of your newspapers."

"And the second?" Hearst asked.

"That it might not affect the circulation."

When Jimmy Carter was elected president in 1976, the press offered hundreds of stories about the new down-home style he would bring to the White House. During the period between Election Day and his inauguration, he and his staff made preparations for the big move. One day, the president-elect and his wife asked the White House chef if they could expect the kind of meals they had always enjoyed.

"Certainly," the chef said. "We've been fixing that kind of food for the servants for years."

Few people in Hollywood doubted that Orson Welles had enormous talent, especially in the days following the release of *Citizen Kane,* which many believe to be the best American film ever made. However, no one had as high an opinion of Welles's talent as the great man himself. Summing up Welles's self-image, Herman Mankiewicz, who co-wrote the screenplay for *Citizen Kane,* pointed to Welles one day and grumbled, "There, but for God, goes God."

. . .

Welles treated his debts with a disdain befitting the
stature he believed was his. When he had allowed one
bill to go unpaid for months, the creditor sent a
telegram: "How will I get along while I am waiting for
the money?"

Welles sent a telegram in reply saying, "Live
simply."

While filming a scene with French actor Alain Delon,
Richard Burton had a close call with an ax that Delon
was swinging over his head. Burton ducked out of the
way, then exclaimed, "Be careful how you handle that
ax! There are plenty of French actors. But if you kill
me, you will have destroyed one-sixth of all the Welsh
actors in the world!"

Author and Union army captain Oliver Wendell Holmes
used to tell a story about the time he was assigned to
escort President Abraham Lincoln on a tour of the front
lines during the Civil War. Pointing to a distant hill, he
told the president that it was occupied by rebel forces.
Lincoln stood up to get a better look and was greeted
by a barrage of gunfire.

Without thinking, Holmes screamed, "Get down, you
fool!" The president quickly obeyed.

Later, when Lincoln was about to leave, he thanked

Holmes for the tour. Then he added, "I'm glad to see you know how to talk to a civilian."

Another story about Lincoln concerns a lawyer—a loyal Republican party worker—who constantly pestered him for an appointment to a Federal judgeship. Lincoln had no faith in the man's abilities, but he softened his refusal by telling him that there were simply no openings to which he could be appointed.

One day, the man saw a body floating in the Potomac River. He pulled the body from the water and realized that the drowned man was a federal judge. He rushed back to the White House with the news.

After telling Lincoln what he had just seen, he said, "So, there is an opening after all."

"I'm sorry," Lincoln said. "You got here too late. I've already appointed the lawyer who saw him fall in."

Fiorello La Guardia was one of the most popular politicians in the history of New York City. After serving in the House of Representatives, he became the city's mayor in 1933 and remained in that office for twelve years. His popularity was based partly on his instinct for public gestures that reflected the feelings of his constituents.

La Guardia once had to deal with the prospect of a high German official visiting New York City, during the years when Hitler and his troops were extending their power. Despite his hatred of the Nazis and the strong anti-Hitler feelings in his city, La Guardia had no choice but to supply police protection for the official. He did, however, find a way of making the gesture that would show how he and other people in the city felt.

He ordered that the bodyguard for the German official be made up of only Jewish policemen.

Director Alfred Hitchcock, who was once quoted as having said, "All actors are cattle," had little regard for the subtleties of what performers did in front of his camera. Acting in one of his movies, Ingrid Bergman once told him that she didn't understand what he was asking her to do.

"I don't think I can do that naturally," she said. She explained why she was having trouble, then listed some other ways that she might play the scene.

Hitchcock listened attentively. When she was finished, he said, "All right. If you can't do it naturally, then fake it."

■

PART FIVE

Sports Jokes and Stories— Some True, Some Possibly True, and Some Not True at All

▲

"In America," columnist Russell Baker has written, "it is sport that is the opiate of the masses." In some daily newspapers, sports news takes up more pages than world, national, and local news combined.

Any topic that important deserves its own section. You shouldn't have any trouble separating truth from fiction here. If you do, follow this rule of thumb: Sports is that one area of American life where just about anything can happen. If it sounds unbelievable, it's very probably true.

▼

Satchel Paige, one of the greatest pitchers in baseball history, spent most of his career in the Negro leagues, before blacks were allowed to play on major league teams. In his seventies, Paige used to hand out business cards that listed his six rules for a happy life:

1. Avoid fried meats, which angry up the blood.
2. If your stomach disputes you, lie down and pacify it with cool thoughts.
3. Keep the juices flowing by jangling around gently as you move.
4. Go very light on vices such as carrying on in society. The social ramble ain't restful.
5. Avoid running at all times.
6. Don't look back. Something might be gaining on you.

Although Camille Henry was one of the smallest players in the National Hockey League, he had a reputation for facing down anyone else in the league, no matter what size. He once tangled with one of the fiercest fighters in hockey. In the middle of the tussle, Henry shouted, "Watch out or I'll bleed all over you!"

. . .

Joe Garagiola tells this story about a day he was catching for the St. Louis Cardinals at Wrigley Field in Chicago. One of the distinguishing features of Wrigley is the ivy that covers the outfield walls. Another is the unpredictable wind, which can create nightmares for even the best of pitchers. On this day, the wind was working very much in the batters' favor, and the Cubs' pitcher was taking a pounding.

Chicago manager Phil Cavaretta walked slowly to the mound, then took the ball from his pitcher. "I hate to take you out," he said consolingly, "but the outfielders are getting poison ivy."

In the middle of his weekly golf match, Kraven stopped and turned to see a funeral cortège driving slowly by on the road outside the golf course. He took off his cap and stood silently while the cars went by. When the last car had passed, he put his cap back on, then proceeded to sink a very difficult putt.

"Congratulations!" his opponent said. "I was sure that funeral cortège was going to ruin your concentration."

"It was a close call," Kraven said. "After all, next month we would have been married for twenty-five years."

. . .

Two visitors from Greece went to a baseball game and sat through five innings. One turned to the other and asked, "Do you have any idea what this game is about?"

No," his friend said. "It's all English to me."

Jeff Cravath, longtime coach of the USC football team, once explained why he gave up coaching to manage his ranch. "Cattle don't have any alumni," he said.

Rube Waddell (1876–1914) is one of those baseball players who are legendary more for their screwball antics than for their performance on the field. Waddell, a pitcher for the Philadelphia Athletics, once stood at bat with a runner on second base and his team trailing by one run.

Waddell watched a pitch go by, and the catcher fired the ball to second in an attempt to pick off the runner. The ball missed the mark and ended up in center field. The alert runner rounded third and headed for home.

By this time, the center fielder had retrieved the ball, and he threw it to the catcher, even though there was no chance at all of nailing the runner. Waddell, still standing in the batter's box, watched the ball sail toward the plate. Then he stepped forward and swung at it.

The ball soared into the air and out of the park. However, Waddell was called out for interfering with the play. When the tumult died down, his infuriated manager asked him why he'd done such a brainless thing.

"They'd been feeding me curves all afternoon," Rube explained. "This was the first straight ball I'd seen."

Casey Stengel is another character who lives on more in story than in the record books. During his days as manager of the New York Mets, Casey was asked to compare Ed Kranepool to another up-and-coming young star. "In ten years," Stengel said, "Kranepool has a chance to be a star. In ten years, the other guy has a chance to be thirty."

During the years when Stengel was their manager, the Mets were the laughingstock of the National League. The player who best exemplified the team's hopelessness was Marv Throneberry, known to the Mets' adoring fans as "Marvelous Marv." Throneberry could be relied on to strike out in any key situation and to make an error just when the opposing team needed it most.

One day, the team held a birthday party for manager Casey Stengel, complete with an enormous birthday cake. Throneberry complained, "How come nobody gave me a cake on my birthday?"

"We would have," Casey said, "but we were afraid you'd drop it."

. . .

"Last week, I devised the perfect system for picking winners at the track."

"Then what happened?"

"The track opened."

Heavyweight champion Jack Dempsey, like most champs, was constantly faced with the problem of drunks challenging him to fights. One night he got a call from the desk clerk of the hotel where he was staying.

"There's a man here who says he can beat you," the clerk said, "and he won't go away."

Dempsey wasn't about to go down and have to deal with the man. So he told the clerk, "Tell him he can have my title. But I want it back in the morning."

Harry Wismer—Hairbreadth Harry—was one of the most famous of the old-time radio sports announcers. Like many of his colleagues, Harry was guilty of occasionally inventing some action to make the game more exciting than it really was. However, even though his audience couldn't see what was happening, they would have the next day's newspapers available to them, so Harry had to maintain some semblance of reality.

In an Army football game, Wismer reported a play in which Doc Blanchard ran seventy yards for a touchdown. The trouble was, Wismer thought it was

Glenn Davis running with the ball. Screaming into his microphone, Wismer reported the phenomenal run Davis was making. Then, when the runner was at the ten-yard line, he realized that it wasn't Davis at all.

"Down to the ten," Wismer screamed. Then, correcting his error in a flash, he said, "And Glenn laterals to Blanchard—touchdown, Blanchard!"

He'd been playing golf for years, and he had the finest equipment, but his technique never improved a bit. As his friend watched, he teed up at the first hole and promptly drove a brand-new ball into the woods. On the second hole, he drove another new ball into a lake. On the third, he lost a new ball in another part of the woods.

"Why don't you use an old ball?" his friend asked.

"I've never had an old ball," he said.

"How is this lake—any good for fish?"

"It must be. I certainly can't persuade any of them to come out."

One time Notre Dame star center Frankie Szymanski once had to appear in court as a witness. Notre Dame coach Frank Leahy was also in the courtroom. As Leahy listened, the following exchange took place.

"Are you on the Notre Dame football team this year?"

"Yes, Your Honor."

"What position do you play?"

"Center, Your Honor."

"How good a center are you?"

Szymanski hesitated. Then he said, "Sir, I'm the best center Notre Dame ever had."

Coach Leahy couldn't believe that last sentence had come out of the mouth of one his most modest players. Afterward, the coach asked his center what had possessed him.

"I hated to do it, Coach," Szymanski said. "But I was under oath."

The pro football team had just finished their daily practice session when a large turkey came strutting onto the field. While the players gaped, the turkey walked up to the head coach and demanded a tryout. They stared in silence as the turkey caught pass after pass and ran right through the defensive line.

When the turkey returned to the sidelines, the coach shouted, "You're terrific! Sign up for the season, and I'll see to it that you get a huge bonus."

"Forget the bonus," the turkey said. "All I want to know is, does the season go past Thanksgiving Day?"

That football coach had a brother who was the manager of the worst semipro baseball team on the eastern seaboard. The team hadn't won a game in six years, and two of their best players were now talking about hanging up their spikes for good. A horse came into the dugout one day and asked the manager for a spot on the team.

"Well," the manager said, "my brother took a chance on a turkey and it paid off. What have I got to lose? You'll be our starting pitcher today."

The horse took the mound in the first inning. He struck out the first batter on three pitches. He did the same to the second and third batters. More astounding than that, he repeated the performance in the second and third innings.

In the bottom of the third, the horse came to bat. He hit a towering fly ball to center field. The ball hit the top of the fence and bounced back onto the field. The center fielder picked it up, dropped it, picked it up again, then fired it into the infield. The ball went sailing over the second baseman's head and got past the catcher. Then the catcher had trouble picking it up. He finally got a grip on it and threw it to the first baseman. The horse was out by ten feet.

He returned to the dugout and sat next to the manager. "You're probably the greatest pitcher I've ever seen," the manager said. "And you can really wallop the ball. But you can't run to save your life."

The horse looked at him. "If I could run," he said, "do you think I'd be here?"

"What's the idea of calling in sick yesterday?"
"I *was* sick."

"You didn't look sick when I saw you at the racetrack."

"You should have seen me after the sixth race."

In 1957, the Milwaukee Braves met the New York Yankees in the World Series. One of the Braves' most fearsome hitters was Henry Aaron, who would go on to become the all-time home run leader in major league history. When he came up to bat, Yankee catcher Yogi Berra did what catchers often do with good hitters—he tried to rattle him.

"You're holding the bat the wrong way," Berra said. "Turn it around so you can see the trademark."

With his eyes steady on the pitcher, Aaron said, "Didn't come up here to read. Came up here to hit."

Bronko Nagurski of the Chicago Bears was one of the biggest—and strongest—men ever to play professional football. On one play from the one-yard line, Nagurski plowed through the defensive line with so much power that he kept going through the end zone. With his head still down, he crashed into a mounted policeman, felling both the cop and his horse.

Not aware of what he'd just done, Nagurski stood up and cleared his head. "That last man hit me awful hard," he said.

• • •

A famous chess master was in the habit of taking his five-year-old son to matches in the hope of instilling a love of the game in the boy. At a tense moment in a championship game, the master reached out to move one of his knights.

"Don't move the horse," the boy said. His father looked at him, thought it over, then decided to make a different move. As a result, he won the game.

Later, he wondered if his son had some kind of intuitive genius for the game of chess. So he asked the boy, "Why did you tell me not to move the horse?"

"He looked tired," the boy said.

In April 1947, Jackie Robinson prepared for opening day at Ebbets Field, where he would become the first black man ever to appear in a major league baseball game. Before he left for the ballpark, he said to his wife Rachel, "If you come today, you won't have any trouble recognizing me."

Then he grinned and added, "My number is 42."

After an astounding college career in the early 1950s, Rodney "Hot Rod" Hundley signed with the Minneapolis Lakers of the National Basketball Association. He and teammate Bob Leonard once missed a team flight because they were out too late the night before. Lakers owner Bob Short had them report to his office the next morning.

Hundley went into Short's office, where he was told

he would be fined a thousand dollars for missing the flight. At 10 percent of Hundley's yearly salary, this was the largest fine ever imposed on a professional basketball player.

Hundley came out of Short's office and was accosted by Leonard, who asked "How much?"

"A big one, baby," Hundley said. "A big bill."

"A hundred dollars?" Leonard asked worriedly.

"A hundred hell," Hundley said. "A thousand."

Leonard gasped. His face fell. He was on the verge of tears. Hundley put his hand on Leonard's shoulder and said, "It's a record."

Leonard's face lit up. "Let's go out and celebrate!"

"What are you watching, Dad?"

"Basketball game."

"What's the score?"

"117 to 114."

"Who's winning?"

"The team with 117."

Ralph Kiner, home run ace for the Pittsburgh Pirates in the days when that team could scarcely win a game, once told this story about the early days of his marriage to former tennis star Nancy Chaffee.

"When I married Nancy," Ralph said, "I vowed I'd beat her at tennis someday. After six months, she beat me 6–2. After a year, she beat me 6–4. After we were married a year and a half, I pushed her to 7–5. Then it happened. She had a bad day, and I had a good one, and I beat her 17–15."

At this point in the story, Kiner was asked if his wife had been sick on that day.

"Of course not!" he said. Then he added, "Well—she *was* eight months pregnant."

Two very old, very retired friends went fishing together. They sat in their boat for four hours, neither of them moving a muscle. An hour later, one friend said to the other, "Damn it, that's the second time you've shifted your feet in the last forty minutes. Did you come out here to fish or to dance?"

In August 1983, the New York Yankees were at Exhibition Stadium for a game against the Toronto Blue Jays. The Yankees had just finished their turn at bat in the fifth inning, and their outfielders were warming up by throwing a ball back and forth. With the Toronto batter about to get up, left fielder Dave Winfield threw the ball in the direction of the Yankee bullpen.

The ball never reached its destination. A sea gull was calmly walking in front of the Yankee bullpen, and Winfield's throw hit the bird straight on.

A ball boy carried the dead bird from the field, and the Toronto fans began acting as though Winfield had just committed murder. They booed loudly and flung garbage at the Yankee fielder.

For a brief moment, the Toronto authorities were swept away by the same silliness that had overtaken the fans. Winfield was placed under arrest after the game and charged with "willfully causing unnecessary cruelty to animals." He had to post a five-hundred-dollar bond in order to be allowed to leave Toronto with the rest of the Yankee team.

The charges were later dropped, of course, but not before the Toronto press had gotten a great deal of mileage out of a pretty insubstantial incident.

Not too surprisingly, Yankee manager Billy Martin had the last word about the affair. "They say Winfield hit the gull on purpose," Martin said. "They wouldn't say that if they could see the throws he's been making all year."

"How many fish have you caught so far?"

"Well, if I catch this one I'm after right now, then catch two more, I'll have three."

Jim Thorpe, possibly the greatest athlete of modern times, won both the decathlon and the pentathlon in the 1912 Olympics. Before winning worldwide fame for this achievement, he was a student at Carlisle University, a school for Indians.

Locally, the Carlisle Indians were known for their outstanding track team. Pop Warner, the Carlisle coach, once received an invitation to compete against nearby

Lafayette College. When the Carlisle team arrived, the Lafayette coach, Harold Anson Bruce, was dumbfounded.

"Where's the rest of your team?" he asked Warner.

"I have all I need," Warner said.

Bruce counted five Carlisle athletes. "But I have forty-six men on my team!" he protested. "We've got eleven events. Your people won't have a chance!"

"We'll see," Warner said.

Two of Warner's runners came in first and second in the half-mile, the mile, and the two-mile races. A third runner won the quarter mile. A fourth won the high hurdles.

Then there was Jim Thorpe. He won the pole vault and the shot put. He took the low hurdles. He placed first in both the broad jump and the high jump. And for good measure, he came in second in the 100-meter race.

Carlisle won the meet 71–31.

Gilbertson had skied every dangerous course from Vermont to Vail, and he was looking for more challenges. He went to Switzerland and sought out the most difficult ski trails he could find. At one ski lodge, he was warned repeatedly not to try a solo run on a certain slope because of the danger of injury.

Gilbertson scoffed at the warnings and took off for the slope. As the Swiss skiers had predicted, he didn't complete his descent. Although he wasn't injured, he ended up in a deep crevasse with no discernible way of getting out. He'd have to get out on his own, however, because he would never admit to the others that he'd met his match.

Hours later, a rescue party spotted him in the crevasse. They called out to let him know he had nothing to worry about. "We're from the Red Cross!"

Determined to maintain his facade, Gilbertson called back, "Sorry, I gave at the office!"

At one time, Tommy Bolt was one of the most famous golfers in the United States. He was known not only for his skill on the greens, but also for his fierce temper. He once had the misfortune of missing six putts in a row by inches. After the sixth miss, he shook his fist at the sky and shouted, "Why don't you come down and fight like a man!"

A golfer, lost somewhere in the rough, asked his caddy, "Why do you keep looking at that pocket watch?"

"It isn't a watch," the caddy said. "It's a compass."

Ty Cobb was undoubtedly one of the best players baseball has ever seen. He will also be remembered as one of the nastiest. One sportswriter said in an obituary of Cobb, "The only difference now is that he is a bad guy who is dead." Cobb was notorious for sliding into second or third base with his spikes high enough to cause serious damage to basemen. Once, he ran into the stands and beat up a fan who had been heckling him. The fan had only one arm.

Even after his playing days were over, Cobb didn't lose his mean streak. When he was sixty years old, he appeared in an old-timers' game. When he came up to the plate, he asked the catcher to move a few steps back, since he didn't trust his old hands to hold onto the bat. The catcher thanked him for the warning and moved back. Then Cobb bunted the next pitch for a base hit.

A not-very-bright boxer stormed into his manager's office one afternoon and slammed his fist on the desk. "Listen to me!" the boxer demanded. "I'm in shape. I've been training for months. I'm in shape, you hear me? For months I've stayed away from sweets and alcohol, I've gotten eight hours' sleep at night, and I've trained and trained and trained. *I'm in shape!* And I want to fight Rocky Polito!"

His manager sat back in his chair and sighed. "If I've told you once," he said, "I've told you a thousand times—you *are* Rocky Polito!"

Los Angeles Dodger Don Sutton was one of those pitchers who are constantly under suspicion of illegally doctoring the ball to gain an advantage over the hitters. Like many other pitchers, Sutton did little to discourage such suspicion, reasoning that if hitters are worried about a spitball, the pitcher already has the necessary advantage.

In the middle of one game, the home plate umpire walked out to the mound and demanded to see Sutton's glove, expecting to find some illegal substance hidden inside. Sutton handed over the glove. Inside, the umpire found a note that read, "You're getting warm, but it's not here."

Champion boxer Rocky Graziano wore his lack of education like a badge. When his boxing days were over and he was trying to make a transition into movies and commercials, someone suggested that he study at the Actors Studio.

"Why should I go to a place like that?" Graziano asked. "All they do is teach guys like Marlon Brando and Paul Newman to talk like me."

As a baseball player, a coach, and a manager, Frankie Frisch never hid his lack of affection for umpires. Once, when Frisch was coaching third base, umpire Bill Klem called a runner out on a close play. Frisch screamed his own interpretation of the play. Then he put his hand to his heart and fell to the ground.

Klem calmly walked over to the fallen coach, who lay on the ground with his eyes closed. "Frisch," Klem said, "dead or alive, you're out of the game."

. . .

Frisch had as much regard for hecklers as he had for
umpires. One day, when he was managing the
Pittsburgh Pirates, he became incensed by a man sitting
right behind the Pirate dugout. The fan screamed at
him throughout the afternoon, offering suggestions on
how the game should be played.

When the game was over, Frisch went into the
stands and asked the man for his name and business
address. The fan was flattered. He gave Frisch the
information, then asked why he wanted it.

Smiling, Frisch replied, "I'll be at your office bright
and early tomorrow morning to tell you how to run
your business."

As manager of the Chicago Cubs, Charlie Grimm
learned as much about losing as anyone who ever wore
a uniform. He developed a wry sense of humor as a
way of dealing with his team's perpetually horrible
situation.

Grimm once got a telephone call from a scout in the
Chicago organization. "I've discovered a great young
pitcher!" the scout said excitedly. "He not only pitched
a perfect game, but he struck out all twenty-seven
batters. Nobody even hit a foul ball until there were
two out in the ninth inning. I've got the pitcher here,
and he's ready to sign. What should I do?"

"Sign up the guy who hit the foul ball," Grimm said.
"We need hitters."

. . .

One of the biggest boxing matches of 1946 was the heavyweight championship rematch between Joe Louis and challenger Billy Conn. Conn was smaller, lighter, and faster than Louis, and the champ's trainers warned him about Conn's tactics.

"He'll attack with a few quick jabs," the champ was told, "then he'll move immediately out of your range."

Louis thought this over and responded, "He can run, but he can't hide."

The guide had been leading the hunting party deeper and deeper into the woods. Finally, he threw up his hands. "We're lost," he said.

One of the members of the hunting party screamed, "Lost? You told me you were the best guide in all of Vermont!"

"I am," the guide said. "But we're in Canada now."

Lefty Gomez was one of the star pitchers of the powerful New York Yankees during the 1930s. Even so, after a very bad year, he was asked to take a cut in pay. Management offered to keep him on if he'd agree to a cut from $20,000 a year down to $8,000.

Gomez was furious, but he remained calm and made a counteroffer. "You keep the salary," he said. "I'll keep the cut."

. . .

Red Auerbach, longtime coach then general manager of
the Boston Celtics, tells this story about his early days
of coaching. He was in a hotel lobby in the early hours
of the morning when he ran into three of his players.
Each player was accompanied by a beautiful young
woman.

One of the players blurted out an introduction,
identifying the woman he was with as his cousin.
Although he realized that this sounded a bit fishy, he
then made matters worse by claiming that they were all
on their way to church.

"I couldn't take that," Auerbach said later. "I fined
him twenty-five dollars for insulting my intelligence."

One of Auerbach's many accomplishments was the
signing of center Bill Russell, who led the Boston
Celtics to eleven championships in thirteen seasons.
This record put Russell far ahead of his career-long
rival, center Wilt Chamberlain. Chamberlain, however,
could boast of being the first NBA player to sign a
$100,000 contract.

Russell's reaction was predictable. For his next
contract, he insisted on receiving $100,001, which
allowed him to crow, "Poor Wilt. Always a dollar short
and a basket late."

. . .

Before the days of free agency, salaries were a constant sore point with professional athletes. Slugger Hank Greenberg once found himself in a salary dispute with Walter Briggs, the owner of the Detroit Tigers.

"You're asking for too much money," Briggs said. "When I was your age, I had two children and was making twenty-five dollars a week."

"That's why I'm asking for so much now," Greenberg said. "When I'm *your* age, *I* could have two children and be making twenty-five dollars a week."

Still on the subject of salaries, there's the story about the time Babe Ruth was asked to take a cut in salary, in recognition of the hard times forced on the team by the Depression. Ruth insisted on the $80,000 he had earned the year before.

A Yankee official pointed out that President Hoover didn't make that much money.

"I know," Ruth said, "but I had a better year."

During Sammy Baugh's years with Washington, the NFL's Redskins were nearly unbeatable. Even so, a game with the Chicago Bears in 1940 turned out to be a disaster for Washington. As the final seconds ticked away, Chicago was leading 73–0. In a desperate attempt to at least avoid a shutout, Baugh led his team down to within one yard of a touchdown. Chicago intercepted his next pass, and the 73–0 score was final.

Afterward, Baugh tried to put the best face on the matter. "If we had gotten that touchdown at the end," he said smiling, "it might have turned the tide."

Sportswriter John Kieran was widely known as a well-educated, well-informed, and literate man. However, his reputation didn't impress the headmaster of a prep school where Kieran was once invited to speak. To the headmaster, the speaker was nothing more than a mere sportswriter. Introducing Kieran to the students, the headmaster pretentiously included a Latin phrase that could be translated as "Let's just make the best of this."

Kieran stood up and said, "Gentlemen, the only thing that outraged me more than the boorishness of the man who introduced me was his inexcusable use of the present participle instead of the past pluperfect in the quotation."

He then went on to give his entire speech in Latin.

"I can't believe it," Marco said. "I haven't had a winning horse in two months!"

"I've been doing well lately," O'Reilly said. "I think it's my new system."

"System?" Marco said. "What system?"

"It's pretty simple, really," O'Reilly said. "Every morning, I go to church and pray for fifteen minutes. Since I started doing that, I haven't had fewer than two winners in a day."

Marco didn't need to be forced. He went to church the next morning and spent thirty minutes praying. Then he went to the track and placed his bets. At the end of the day, he ran into O'Reilly.

"That system of yours didn't work," Marco said. "I went to church this morning. Not a single winner all day."

"You went to church this morning?" O'Reilly said. "Where?"

"The one on Apple Street," Marco said.

"You jerk," O'Reilly said. "That church is for the trotters!"

Show-business celebrities have a well-known addiction to golf, although their aspirations often exceed their skill. Frank Sinatra once played eighteen holes with golf pro Arnold Palmer. Afterward, Sinatra asked, "What do you think of my game?"

"It's not bad," Palmer said, "but I still prefer golf."

Jackie Gleason was another entertainer who was an avid golfer. He once introduced his friend Toots Shor to the game, and Shor racked up a miserable 211. After the game, he asked Gleason, "What do you think I should give the caddy?"

"Your clubs," Gleason said.

. . .

For all anyone knows, it might have been Shor and Gleason who had the following exchange:

"My doctor tells me I can't play golf."

"So he's played with you, too, eh?"

The Texan and the Alaskan were trying to outdo each other with claims about—what else?—size. "I caught a fish last week," the Alaskan said, "that measured a full ten inches."

"What?" laughed the Texan. "Why, that's tiny!"

"In Alaska," his companion said, "we measure between the eyes."

Fred came running up to the hunting campsite, out of breath. "Harry," he said panting, "are all the guys out of the woods yet?"

"Yes," Harry said.

"All six of them?"

"Yes."

"And everybody's safe?"

"Yes," Harry said.

"In that case," Fred said proudly, "I've just shot a deer!"

Three big-game hunters in Africa were resting at their campsite after a difficult day. Parker stood up and stretched. "I think I'll go for a short walk before dinner," he said.

An hour later, he hadn't returned. One of his companions asked the other, "I wonder what's eating Parker?"

Americans are people who wonder why other countries resent us—and think nothing of calling it the World Series.

One result of the scandal surrounding the throwing of the 1919 World Series by several members of the Chicago Black Sox was the creation of the office of Commissioner of Baseball. Chosen as the man to oversee the morals and ethics of those who took part in major league baseball was the imperious Judge Kenesaw Mountain Landis. Some said Landis looked like God—the fearsome, gray-haired deity of the Old Testament.

In court, Landis once sentenced a repeat offender to five years. The man protested. "I'll be dead before I serve that sentence, Your Honor," he said. "I'm a sick man. I can't do five years."

Landis tightened his bushy gray eyebrows and peered down at the man. "You can try, can't you?" he boomed.

In 1902, British heavyweight Robert Fitzsimmons was scheduled to fight American champion James J. Jeffries. Jeffries had the advantage in height, weight, and overall bulk, and Fitzsimmons was asked how he felt about this situation.

He replied, "The bigger they are, the harder they fall."

Hall-of-Fame pitcher Dizzy Dean was known for the dozens of serious (though not fatal) injuries he inflicted on the English language. An interviewer once reported to him that he had been publicly accused of doing damage to young people with his devil-may-care grammar.

Dean thought for a few seconds. Then he said, "A lot of people who don't say 'ain't' ain't eating."

Muhammad Ali held the heavyweight boxing title for a total of thirteen years over a sixteen-year stretch. During his reign, he was known for the verbal jousting he subjected his opponents to before each bout.

Ali went to see the movie *Rocky II,* which, like its predecessor, featured a boxer modeled pretty closely on Ali. In one scene, this character jeers at Rocky and announces, "I'll destroy you. I am the master of disaster."

After watching the film, Ali said, " 'Master of disaster.' Why didn't I think of that!"

■ ■ ■

PART SIX

Quotable Quips

▲

This section is our answer to Bartlett's Familiar Quotations *and all its esteemed imitators. We've culled a collection of quotes guaranteed to bring anything from a smile to a guffaw from even the most hardened listeners. The alphabetical listing of topics will make it easy for you to find what you need.*

▼

• *Advice* •

Advice is worth what it costs—that is, nothing.
—*Douglas MacArthur*

The only thing to do with good advice is to pass it on;
it is never of any use to oneself.   —*Oscar Wilde*

When a man comes to me for advice, I find out the
kind of advice he wants, and I give it to him.
—*Josh Billings*

In those days, he was wiser than he is now. He used
frequently to take my advice.   —*Winston Churchill*

Give me money, not advice.   —*Portuguese proverb*

Old people like to give good advice, as solace for no
longer being able to provide bad examples.
—*François, duc de La Rochefoucauld*

• *Age* •

Youth is the best time to be rich and the best time to be poor.　　　　　　　　　　　　—*Euripides*

Never trust anyone over thirty.　　　—*Abbie Hoffman*

Everything I know I learned after I was thirty.
　　　　　　　　　　　—*Georges Clemenceau*

When I was eighteen, I wanted to save the world. Now, I'd be happy to save a hundred dollars.　　—*Earl Wilson*

God help us if the younger generation ever stops being the despair of its grandparents.　　—*Deems Taylor*

I am not young enough to know everything.
　　　　　　　　　　　　—*James M. Barrie*

Youth is a wonderful thing. What a crime to waste it on children.　　　　　　　　　—*George Bernard Shaw*

Men who are "orthodox" when they are young are in
danger of being middle-aged all their lives.
—*Walter Lippmann*

Middle age is when you're sitting at home on a
Saturday night and the telephone rings and you hope it
isn't for you.   —*Ogden Nash*

From middle age on, everything of interest is either
illegal, immoral, or fattening.   —*Alexander Woollcott*

When you are slowed down by the doctor instead of
the police, you have reached middle age. —*Anonymous*

Middle age: When you begin to exchange your
emotions for symptoms.   —*Irvin S. Cobb*

Grow up as soon as you can. It pays. The only time
you really live fully is from thirty to sixty.
—*Hervey Allen*

Longevity is one of the more dubious rewards of virtue.
—*Ngaio Marsh*

At seventy, one is no longer on the threshold of old age. One is just an old man.   —*W. Somerset Maugham*

To me, old age is always fifteen years older than I am.
—*Bernard Baruch*

That sign of old age, extolling the past at the expense of the present.   —*Sydney Smith*

The older I grow, the more I distrust the familiar doctrine that age brings wisdom.   —*H. L. Mencken*

• *Appearance* •

It is an interesting question how far men would retain their relative rank if they were divested of their clothes.   —*Henry David Thoreau*

I hate to see men overdressed; a man ought to look like he's put together by accident, not added up on purpose.   —*Christopher Morley*

If we could see ourselves as others see us, we might never come back for a second look.   —*Anonymous*

Common-looking people are the best in the world. That
is the reason the Lord made so many of them.

—*Abraham Lincoln*

• *Arts* •

Art is a collaboration between God and the artist, and
the less the artist does the better.   —*André Gide*

Publishing a volume of poetry is like dropping a rose
petal down the Grand Canyon and waiting for the echo.

—*Don Marquis*

The difference between the almost right word and the
right word . . . [is] the difference between the lightning
bug and the lightning.   —*Mark Twain*

A well-written life is almost as rare as a well-spent one.

—*Thomas Carlyle*

There's nothing to writing. All you do is sit down at a
typewriter and open a vein.   —*Red Smith*

If Botticelli were alive today, he'd be working for
Vogue.   —*Peter Ustinov*

• *Business* •

When a person with experience meets a person with money, the person with experience will get the money. And the person with the money will get some experience.
—*Leonard Lauder*

The trouble with the profit system has always been that it was highly unprofitable to most people. —*E. B. White*

When two men in a business always agree, one of them is unnecessary.
—*William Wrigley, Jr.*

It is not the crook in modern business that we fear, but the honest man who doesn't know what he is doing.
—*Owen D. Young*

A verbal contract isn't worth the paper it's printed on.
—*Samuel Goldwyn*

• *Children* •

Before I got married, I had six theories about bringing up children. Now I have six children, and no theories.
—*John Wilmot, earl of Rochester*

By the time the youngest children have learned to keep the house tidy, the oldest grandchildren are on hand to tear it to pieces again. —*Christopher Morley*

Chilren have more need of models than of critics. —*Joseph Joubert*

Pretty much all the honest truth-telling there is in the world is done by children. —*Oliver Wendell Holmes*

It now costs more to amuse a child than it once did to educate either of his parents. —*Anonymous*

Parents were invented to keep children happy by giving them something to ignore. —*Ogden Nash*

• *Death* •

I never wanted to see anybody die, but there are a few obituary notices I have read with pleasure.
—*Clarence Darrow*

In the long run, we are all dead.
—*John Maynard Keynes*

Nothing is as certain as death and taxes. However, death isn't an annual event. —*Anonymous*

• *Economics* •

It's called political economy because it has nothing to do with either politics or economy. —*Stephen Leacock*

If all economists were laid end to end, they would not reach a conclusion. —*George Bernard Shaw*

The one comforting feature of being an economist is that no one else can predict the future either.
—*Anonymous*

Recession is when your neighbor loses his job. Depression is when you lose yours. —*Harry S Truman*

A study of economics usually reveals that the best time to buy anything is last year. —*Marty Allen*

I learned more about economics from one South Dakota dust storm than I did in all my years in college.
—*Hubert Humphrey*

• *Education* •

Soap and education are not as sudden as a massacre, but they are more deadly in the long run.

—*Mark Twain*

I have never let my schooling interfere with my education.

—*Mark Twain*

Education: That which discloses to the wise and disguises from the foolish their lack of understanding.

—*Ambrose Bierce*

I respect faith, but doubt is what gets you an education.

—*Wilson Mizner*

I find honorary degrees always tempting, and often bad for me: tempting because we all—even ex-politicians—hope to be mistaken for scholars, and bad because if you then make a speech, the mistake is exposed.

—*Adlai E. Stevenson*

He who teaches often learns himself.   —*Italian proverb*

Training is everything. The peach was once a bitter almond; cauliflower is nothing but cabbage with a college education.
—*Mark Twain*

• *Experience* •

The only thing experience teaches us is that experience teaches us nothing.
—*André Maurois*

Experience is the name everyone gives to their mistakes.
—*Oscar Wilde*

A rolling stone gathers no moss, but it gains a certain polish.
—*Oliver Herford*

An optimist is a guy that has never had much experience.
—*Don Marquis*

• *Fame* •

Fame is delightful, but as collateral it does not rank high.
—*Elbert Hubbard*

I had rather men should ask why no statue has been erected in my honor than why one has. —*Cato*

Fame is proof that the people are gullible.
—*Ralph Waldo Emerson*

It took me fifteen years to discover I had no talent for writing, but I couldn't give it up because by that time I was famous. —*Robert Benchley*

A sign of a celebrity is often that his name is worth more than his services. —*Daniel Boorstin*

The fact that people do not understand and respect the very best things, such as Mozart's concertos, is what permits men like us to become famous.
—*Johannes Brahms*

• *Fashion* •

Fashion: A despot whom the wise ridicule and obey.
—*Ambrose Bierce*

Fashion is a form of ugliness so intolerable that we have to alter it every six months. —*Oscar Wilde*

Every generation laughs at the old fashions but follows
religiously the new.　　　　　　　　*—Henry David Thoreau*

• *Friends* •

Most people enjoy the inferiority of their best friends.
　　　　　　　—Philip Stanhope, earl of Chesterfield

Laughter is not a bad beginning for a friendship, and it
is the best ending for one.　　　　　　　*—Oscar Wilde*

A real friend is one who walks in when the rest of the
world walks out.　　　　　　　*—Walter Winchell*

Of all cold words of tongue or pen
The worst are these: "I knew him when."
　　　　　　　　　　　—Arthur Guiterman

• *Genius* •

Talent may in time be forgiven, but genius never.
　　　　　　　—George Gordon, Lord Byron

A genius is a man who has *two* great ideas.
　　　　　　　　　　　—Jacob Bronowski

Genius is an African who dreams up snow.
— *Vladimir Nabokov*

When a true genius appears in the world, you may know him by this sign, that the dunces are all in confederacy against him.   — *Jonathan Swift*

• *Honesty* •

Honesty is for the most part less profitable than dishonesty.   — *Plato*

Honesty pays, but it doesn't pay enough to suit most people.   — *Frank M. Hubbard*

If you do not tell the truth about yourself, you cannot tell it about other people.   — *Virginia Woolf*

There's one way to find out if a man is honest. Ask him. If he says yes, you know he's a crook.
— *Groucho Marx*

The louder he talked of his honesty, the faster we counted our spoons.   — *Ralph Waldo Emerson*

• *Humor* •

Comedy is simply a funny way of being serious.
—*Peter Ustinov*

Everything is funny as long as it is happening to somebody else. —*Will Rogers*

You can pretend to be serious, but you can't pretend to be witty. —*Sacha Guitry*

It's hard to be funny when you have to be clean.
—*Mae West*

A pun is the lowest form of humor—when you don't think of it first. —*Oscar Levant*

Man thinks; God laughs. —*Yiddish proverb*

• *Insults* •

She ran the whole gamut of emotions from A to B.
—*Dorothy Parker on Katharine Hepburn*

California is a great place to live, if you happen to be an orange.
—*Fred Allen*

Perfectly Scandalous was one of those plays in which all of the actors unfortunately enunciated very clearly.
—*Robert Benchley*

I went to Philadelphia one Sunday. The place was closed.
—*W. C. Fields*

A day away from Tallulah [Bankhead] is like a month in the country.
—*Howard Dietz*

The reason so many people turned up at [Louis B. Mayer's] funeral is that they wanted make sure he was dead.
—*Samuel Goldwyn*

Sam [Goldwyn] is the only man in the world who can throw a seven with one die.
—*Chico Marx*

I always said that I'd like [John] Barrymore's acting till the cows came home. Well, ladies and gentlemen, last night the cows came home.
—*George Jean Nathan*

Any man who hates dogs and babies can't be all bad.
—*Leo Rosten on W. C. Fields*

I am watching your performance from the rear of the house. Wish you were here.
—*George S. Kaufman in a telegram to an actor performing in one of his plays*

• *Justice* •

There is no such thing as justice—in or out of court.
—*Clarence Darrow*

A judge is a law student who marks his own examination papers. —*H. L. Mencken*

A jury consists of twelve persons chosen to decide who has the better lawyer. —*Robert Frost*

Love of justice in most men is no more than the fear of suffering injustice.
—*François, duc de La Rochefoucauld*

There are many . . . who hold that things break even for all of us. I have observed, for example, that we all get the same amount of ice. The rich get it in the summertime, and the poor get it in the winter.

—*Bat Masterson*

• *Life* •

Life is one long process of getting fired.

—*Samuel Butler*

Life is just one damned thing after another.

—*Frank Ward O'Malley (also attributed to Elbert Hubbard)*

It is not true that life is one damned thing after another—it is one damned thing over and over.

—*Edna St. Vincent Millay*

Life is a foreign language. All men mispronounce it.

—*Christopher Morley*

Life is like eating artichokes. You've got to go through so much to get so little.

—*T. A. Dorgan*

• *Love and Marriage* •

Men always want to be a woman's first love. Women have a more subtle instinct: what they like is to be a man's last romance.　　　　　　　*—Oscar Wilde*

Love is the triumph of imagination over intelligence.
　　　　　　　　　　　　　　　　—H. L. Mencken

Marriage: A community consisting of a master, a mistress, and two slaves, making in all, two.
　　　　　　　　　　　　　　　—Ambrose Bierce

Love is said to be blind, but I know lots of fellows in love who can see twice as much in their sweethearts as I can.　　　　　　　　　　　　*—Josh Billings*

Keep the eyes open before marriage and half-shut afterward.　　　　　　　　　　*—Thomas Fuller*

The conception of two people living together for twenty-five years without having a cross word suggests a lack of spirit to be admired only in sheep.
　　　　　　　　　　　　　　　　—A. P. Herbert

• *Media* •

The printing press is either the greatest blessing or the greatest curse of modern times, one sometimes forgets which.
—*James M. Barrie*

The most truthful part of a newspaper is the advertisements.
—*Thomas Jefferson*

News: The first rough draft of history.   —*Ben Bradlee*

Television is called a medium because it is neither rare nor well done.
—*Ernie Kovacs*

Television is chewing gum for the eyes.   —*Fred Allen*

• *Money* •

When money talks, there are few interruptions.
—*Herbert V. Prochnow*

Certainly there are lots of things in life that money
can't buy, but it's very funny—
Have you ever tried to buy them without money?
—*Ogden Nash*

Lack of money is the root of all evil.
—*George Bernard Shaw*

There are no pockets in a shroud.   —*Yiddish proverb*

A too-constant preoccupation with money may seem to
indicate the lack of a proper sense of moral values, but
[let] those who have always had money . . . be without
it for a while, and they will soon discover how quickly
it becomes their chief concern.   —*Moss Hart*

Money: A blessing that is of no advantage to us
excepting when we part with it.   —*Ambrose Bierce*

Every man thinks God is on his side. The rich and
powerful know he is.   —*Jean Anouilh*

It is very difficult for the prosperous to be humble.
—*Jane Austen*

A penny will hide the biggest star in the universe if you hold it close enough to your eye.   —*Samuel Grafton*

I don't like money actually, but it quiets my nerves.
—*Joe Louis*

Those who set out to serve both God and Mammon soon discover that there is no God.
—*Logan Pearsall Smith*

A billion here and a billion there, and pretty soon you're talking big money.   —*Everett Dirksen*

Virtue has never been as respectable as money.
—*Mark Twain*

Money is a singular thing. It ranks with love as man's greatest source of joy. And with death as his greatest source of anxiety.   —*John Kenneth Galbraith*

When a man tells you he got rich through hard work, ask him, "Whose?"   —*Don Marquis*

His money is twice tainted. 'Taint yours and 'taint mine.
—*Mark Twain*

• *Politics* •

Persistence in one opinion has never been considered a merit in political leaders. —*Cato*

There is no more independence in politics than there is in jail. —*Will Rogers*

My country has in its wisdom contrived for me the most insignificant office that ever the invention of man contrived or his imagination conceived.
—*John Adams on the vice presidency*

The politicians were talking themselves red, white, and blue in the face. —*Clare Boothe Luce*

Since a politician never believes what he says, he is surprised when others believe him. —*Charles de Gaulle*

A statesman is any politician it's considered safe to name a school after. —*Bill Vaughan*

Politics is perhaps the only profession for which no preparation is thought necessary.
—*Robert Louis Stevenson*

A man who is not a liberal at sixteen has no heart. A man who is not a conservative at sixty has no head.
— *Benjamin Disraeli*

• *Procrastination* •

Work is the greatest thing in the world, so we should always save some of it for tomorrow.   — *Don Herold*

He who hesitates is sometimes saved. — *James Thurber*

Procrastination is the art of keeping up with yesterday.
— *Don Marquis*

Never put off till tomorrow what you can do the day after tomorrow just as well.   — *Mark Twain*

• *Sex* •

If your life at night is good, you think you have everything.   — *Euripides*

The bed is the poor man's opera.   — *Italian proverb*

You mustn't force sex to do the work of love, or love
to do the work of sex.   —*Mary McCarthy*

As I grow older
And totter toward the tomb,
I find I care less and less
Who goes to bed with whom.   —*Dorothy L. Sayers*

The ability to make love frivolously is the chief
characteristic which distinguishes human beings from
beasts.   —*Heywood Broun*

Contraceptives should be used on all conceivable
occasions.   —*Spike Milligan*

• *Technology* •

Technological progress has merely provided us with
more efficient means of going backward.
                          —*Robert Maynard Hutchins*

To err is human. But in order to really foul things up,
you need a computer.   —*Anonymous*

The real problem is not whether machines think, but whether men do. —*B. F. Skinner*

I have always considered that the substitution of the internal combustion engine for the horse marked a very gloomy milestone in the progress of mankind.
—*Winston Churchill*

Any sufficiently advanced technology is indistinguishable from magic. —*Arthur C. Clarke*

What we call progress is the exchange of one nuisance for another nuisance. —*Havelock Ellis*

In the past, human life was lived in a bullock cart; in the future, it will be lived in an aeroplane; and the change of speed amounts to a difference in quality.
—*Alfred North Whitehead*

Is it progress if a cannibal uses a fork? —*Stanislaw Lem*

• *Trouble* •

I believe in getting into hot water. It keeps you clean.
—*G. K. Chesterton*

Problems are only opportunities in work clothes.
—*Henry J. Kaiser*

There is nothing so consoling as to find that one's neighbor's troubles are at least as great as one's own.
—*George Moore*

I am an old man and have known a great many troubles, but most of them never happened.
—*Mark Twain*

If you can keep your head when all about you are losing theirs, it is just possible that you haven't grasped the situation.
—*Jean Kerr*

If a man could have half his wishes, he would double his troubles.
—*Benjamin Franklin*

• *Virtue* •

In my experience, good deeds usually do not go unpunished.
—*William Sloane Coffin*

Virtue would not go to such lengths if vanity did not keep her company.—*François, due de La Rochefoucauld*

I think mankind by thee would be less bored
If only thou wert not thine own reward.   —*J. K. Bangs*

Always do right. This will gratify some people and astonish the rest.   —*Mark Twain*

• *Winning and Losing* •

Winning is overemphasized. The only time it is really important is in surgery and war.   —*Al McGuire*

'Tis better to have loved and lost than never to have lost at all.   —*Samuel Butler*

Nice guys finish last.   —*Leo Durocher*

Victory has a thousand fathers, but defeat is an orphan.
                                                    —*John F. Kennedy*

I do not think that winning is the most important thing. I think winning is the only thing.
> —*Bill Veeck (If Vince Lombardi ever said it at all, he didn't say it first.)*

• *Wisdom* •

If a man empties his purse into his head, no one can take it from him.
> —*Benjamin Franklin*

Be wiser than other people if you can, but do not tell them so.
> —*Philip Stanhope, earl of Chesterfield*

He who devotes sixteen hours a day to hard study may become as wise at sixty as he thought himself at twenty.
> —*Mary Wilson Little*

• *Work* •

One machine can do the work of fifty ordinary men. No machine can do the work of one extraordinary man.
> —*Elbert Hubbard*

Working people have a lot of bad habits, but the worst of them is work. —*Clarence Darrow*

Farming looks mighty easy when your plow is a pencil and you're a thousand miles from a cornfield.
—*Dwight D. Eisenhower*

Work expands so as to fill the time available for its completion. —*C. Northcote Parkinson*

In a hierarchy, every employee tends to rise to his level of incompetence. —*Laurence J. Peter*

PART SEVEN

▪ ■ ▪

The End

▲

Are there topics that are so ghastly that they simply can't be made funny?

Yes, there probably are.

Is death one of those topics?

Don't be silly.

We decided to close the book with some graveyard humor because death just may be the funniest topic of them all.

▼

First, some words of remembrance taken from real tombstones:

Here lies the body of William Gray,
Who died defending his right-of-way.
He was right—dead right—as he sped along,
But he's just as dead as if he'd been wrong.

Here lies Martin Elmerod.
Have mercy on my soul, good God,
As I would do were I Lord God
And you were Martin Elmerod.

In a Vermont cemetery, a stone expresses the thoughts
of a widow after her husband was buried:
Rest in peace—until we meet again.

Here lies the body of our Anna,
Done to death by a banana.
It wasn't the fruit that laid her low
But the skin of the thing that made her go.

Next, a collection of epitaphs some people have suggested for themselves:

W. C. Fields: On the whole, I'd rather be in Philadelphia.

Actor Wallace Ford: At last, I get top billing.

Dentist Horace Brown:
Stranger, approach these bones with gravity.
Doc Brown is filling his last cavity.

Writer Dorothy Parker: Excuse my dust.

Actress Hedy Lamarr: This is too deep for me.

Pianist (and world-class hypochondriac) Oscar Levant: I *told* you I was sick.

And finally, the actual, documented last words of a handful of people who refused to be overly solemn about their last moments:

. . .

The Reverend Henry Ward Beecher (1813–1887), after being asked by his doctor how high he could raise his arm: "Well, high enough to hit you, Doctor."

Philosopher Georg Wilhelm Hegel (1770–1831): "Only one man ever understood me. And *he* didn't understand me."

Author Oscar Wilde (1854–1900), after asking for a glass of champagne: "I am dying as I have lived—beyond my means."

John Henry "Doc" Holliday (1852–1887), dentist, gambler, sometime gunman, and friend of Wyatt Earp, after awakening from a coma and learning that he was dying of TB and not of a gun shot: "This is funny!"

Philosopher Auguste Comte (1798–1857): "What an irreparable loss!"

Humorist Robert Benchley (1889–1945), in a marginal note on the article he was reading, entitled "Am I Thinking?": "No. (And supposing you were?)"

. . .

Grammarian Dominique Bouhours (1628–1702): "I am about to—or I am going to—die. Either expression is used."

Historian Thomas Carlyle (1795–1881): "So this is death. Well. . . ."

• *Index* •

(continued)

P. D. James, *The Children of Men*
Naomi Judd, *Love Can Build a Bridge* (paper)
Dean Koontz, *Dark Rivers of the Heart* (paper)
Judith Krantz, *Dazzle*
Judith Krantz, *Lovers* (paper)
John le Carré, *The Night Manager* (paper)
John le Carré, *The Secret Pilgrim*
Robert Ludlum, *The Bourne Ultimatum*
Cormac McCarthy, *The Crossing* (paper)
Audrey Meadows with Joe Daley, *Love, Alice* (paper)
James A. Michener, *Mexico* (paper)
James A. Michener, *The Novel*
James A. Michener, *Recessional* (paper)
James A. Michener, *The World Is My Home* (paper)
Sherwin B. Nuland, *How We Die* (paper)
Richard North Patterson, *Degree of Guilt*
Louis Phillips, editor, *The Random House Large Print
        Treasury of Best-Loved Poems*
Maria Riva, *Marlene Dietrich* (2 volumes, paper)
Margaret Truman, *Murder at the National Cathedral*
Margaret Truman, *Murder at the Pentagon*
Margaret Truman, *Murder on the Potomac* (paper)
Anne Tyler, *Saint Maybe*
John Updike, *Rabbit at Rest*
Phyllis A. Whitney, *Daughter of the Stars* (paper)
Phyllis A. Whitney, *Star Flight* (paper)
Lois Wyse, *Grandchildren Are So Much Fun
        I Should Have Had Them First*

———————————

The New York Times Large Print Crossword Puzzles (paper)

Will Weng, editor, Volumes 1–3
Eugene T. Maleska, editor, Volumes 4–7
Eugene T. Maleska, editor, Omnibus Volume 1